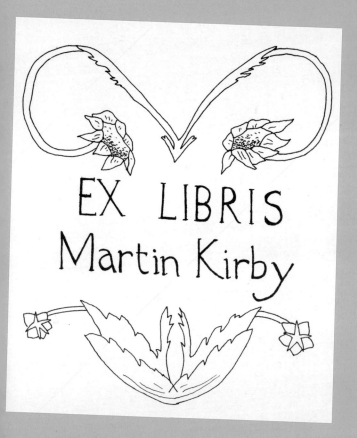

EX LIBRIS
Martin Kirby

SMALL *Oxford* BOOKS

THE COUNTRY HOUSE

SMALL *Oxford* BOOKS

THE COUNTRY HOUSE

Compiled by
JAMES LEES-MILNE

Oxford New York
OXFORD UNIVERSITY PRESS
1982

Oxford University Press, Walton Street, Oxford OX2 6DP

London Glasgow New York Toronto
Delhi Bombay Calcutta Madras Karachi
Kuala Lumpur Singapore Hong Kong Tokyo
Nairobi Dar es Salaam Cape Town
Melbourne Auckland

and associates in
Beirut Berlin Ibadan Mexico City Nicosia

Compilation, introduction, and editorial matter
© *James Lees-Milne 1982*

British Library Cataloguing in Publication Data

The Country house.—(Small Oxford books)
1. Country homes—Great Britain—History
2. Great Britain—Social life and customs
I. Lees-Milne, James
941.0092′2 DA115

ISBN 0-19-214139-2

Library of Congress Cataloging in Publication Data

Lees-Milne, James.
The country house.
(Small Oxford books)
Includes index.
1. England—Social life and customs—20th
century. 2. Country life—England. 3. Country
homes—England. I. Title.
DA566.4.L38 942 82-2092
ISBN 0-19-214139-2 AACR2

Set by Western Printing Services Ltd.
Printed in Great Britain by
Hazell Watson & Viney Limited
Aylesbury, Bucks

Introduction

Fifty years ago (which to some of us seems but yesterday) an anthology such as this would have been considered grotesque. It would have made no more sense than an anthology of flats and flat life – which may well be undertaken fifty years hence when human beings are again reduced to inhabiting caves. In fact until the outbreak of the last war the English country house, although admittedly under threat, was still the recognized dwelling place of upper-class families. Little interest therefore was evoked by it, and absolutely none by the life that went on within and around it. Today the English country house way of life is in retrospect second in popularity only to Bloomsbury. Now whereas the Bloomsberries died a natural death, the county families have been liquidated by the State with calculated thoroughness.

One of the many contradictory qualities of the British is to revere, and even lament, the things they are in the process of destroying. Country houses therefore share the same veneration as the English landscape – once the most beautiful in Europe – English villages, English trees, English wild life and wild flowers, and all those other delectable English things which commercial tycoons, government contractors, and farmers are systematically eliminating by means of rural factories, housing estates, power stations, motorways, pesticides and the burning every August and September of arable fields and hedgerows.

Dozens of books about country houses and the archaic species who resided in them are published annually, often at vast expense. Avidly they are read and copiously are crocodile tears shed over the melancholy conditions which they describe. Indeed the subject is so various that there is no reason why it should ever, unlike Bloomsbury, be exhausted. For whereas the last group was confined to a select few of a single generation living within a circumscribed zone, the archaic species I have just referred to existed for some five hundred years and was spread over the whole smiling face of the British Isles.

To compile an anthology of the English Country House and its way of life within 100 small pages is not unlike attempting to write the history of the world on the proverbial sixpence. Quite apart from the mountain of literature about domestic architecture, decoration, furniture, pictures, etc., there is an abundance of printed memoirs, diaries and correspondence written by English and foreign country-house visitors of the past. The task of elimination and condensation has accordingly been daunting. So I must hope to enlist sympathy rather than recrimination from the disappointed browser of the following pages when he misses extracts from his favourite chroniclers and references to his favourite houses. Fully aware too that there are infinite facets to the country house, I have perforce confined my quotations to twenty-six headings, arbitrarily chosen and of course inadequately covered. I have endeavoured to arrange the quotations chronologically; that is to say, in relation to the date of the event recorded, if it is an event, or the description, if it is a description, rather than the date of the publication from which it is taken. The publication, with the author's name, is in each case subjoined.

Even so some of my quotations will be familiar. I make no apology for this because their very familiarity means that they are good quotations. I have included a few from fiction where these convey a contemporary picture of the country-house setting, but none from Disraeli's novels. Of all English novelists he was the most besotted by grand country houses. But his lengthy descriptions of their architecture and ambience are totally unhistoric. He had no eye for style. To him all country houses were either feudal fortresses (modernized) or 'italianate' palaces, enormous, opulent and ornate, their 'capacious chambers' resplendent with 'Venetian' gold, set in parks where fallow deer tripped among ferny solitudes. Far more convincing are the impressionistic sketches left us by novelists like Jane Austen and George Eliot, who were sparing with their casual references.

Two interesting conclusions struck me in the course of this compilation. How critical the eighteenth-century commentators were of the houses of their own time. Whereas we are inclined to think Georgian builders could never put a foot wrong Georgian visitors seldom seemed to think they ever put one right. Blue-stocking Mrs Montagu made mock of the 'Frenchified' decoration of Lord Baltimore's Woodcote Park, and William Cobbett had not a good word to say for Mrs Montagu's Sandleford Priory. Sarah Haslam positively inveighed against the 'quimp & crank . . . & extravagant foolery' of the neo-Gothic style. And Lord Torrington, admittedly no aesthete, detested classical elegance. He poured scorn on what he called the 'frippery' of the Adam brothers' decoration, which even Horace Walpole, who *was* an aesthete, was not beyond criticizing. In fact, it was carp, carp, carp all along the line. Which merely goes to show that our ancestors had higher standards of taste than our own.

My second conclusion was that the country way of life in 1932 approximated more nearly to that of 1732 than it does to that of 1982. Fifty years ago country houses were still the active capitals of little principalities. Servants' halls were populated. Stables were full of horses; gardens of gardeners. During mornings the purlieus were buzzing with life. On summer afternoons however the golden stillness was disturbed only by a pony-drawn mowing machine; in summer evenings by the lazy pat of tennis balls or the somnolent click of croquet mallets. Beyond the park wall the distant escarpment of the estate was unbroken by regiments of electricity pylons. Nature was uncontaminated. Man was still her partner, and not her exploiter. He fashioned her, he trimmed her, but he cherished her. The natural environment was part and parcel of the country-house scene.

J.L-M.

To my further great benefit, as I grew older, I thus saw nearly all the noblemen's houses in England; in reverent and healthy delight of uncovetous admiration – perceiving, as soon as I could perceive any political truth at all, that it was probably much happier to live in a small house, and have Warwick Castle to be astonished at, than to live in Warwick Castle and have nothing to be astonished at; but that, at all events, it would not make Brunswick Square in the least more pleasantly habitable, to pull Warwick Castle down.

John Ruskin, *Praeterita*, Vol. I, ch. I. vi, 1885–9

The house stamps its own character on all ways of living: I am ruled by a continuity that I cannot see.

Elizabeth Bowen, *Bowen's Court*, 1942

Where great landlords are secure, there is less danger to the landscape pattern. From end to end of England wherever you meet seemly villages and a countryside that speaks of understanding and affection, the chances are that you will be on a large estate.

Robin Fedden, *The Continuing Purpose*, 1968

Building

The motives for are followed by the process of building a country house.

Rural scenery is so congenial to the human mind, that there are few persons who do not indulge the hope of retiring at some period into the country.

J. Loudon, On Country Residences, Vol. 1, 1806

Houses are built to live in, and not to look on; therefore let use be preferred before uniformity, except where both may be had. . . . You shall have sometimes fair houses so full of glass, that one cannot tell where to become to be out of the sun or cold.

Francis Bacon, Of Building, 1625

In the following case impulse forestalled forethought :

Wimbledon House, Surrey : The House built for the old Duchess of Marlbro, by Henry Earl of Pembroke. She would have it sunk in a fossé, and then said, it looked as if it was making a Curtsie.

Horace Walpole, Visits to Country Seats, 1751

Another safety-valve that the gentry of the old school had for emitting the steam of their wealth, besides keeping hounds and electioneering, was in huge house-building – they built against each other. If Squire Fatfield built a great staring house, Squire Flaggon would follow suit with a bigger, and Squire Jollybuck would cap Squire Flaggon with a larger still. Now building a big house, and buying a big house, are two distinct things; for the builder of a big house is expected to live in it, and maintain a suitable establishment, while the buyer of a big house can shut up as much of it as he finds is too large for his purpose.

R. S. Surtees, *Plain or Ringlets*, 1860

Architects and Clients

It is hard to decide which of the two finds the other more unsatisfactory.

I have always had the misfortune to suffer very great mischiefs from the assistance of architects.

Sarah, Duchess of Marlborough, *Correspondence*, 5.8.1734

Madam, When I writ to your Grace on Tuesday last I was much at a loss, what cou'd be the ground of your having drop't me in the service I had been endeavouring to do you and your family with the Duke of Newcastle, Upon your sole Motion and desire. But having since been shewn by Mr Richards a large packet of building papers sent him by your Grace, I find the reason was, That you had resolv'd to use me so ill in respect of Blenheim, as must make it Impracticable to employ me in any other Branch of your service. These papers Madam are so full of far-fetched Labour'd Accusations, Mistaken Facts, Wrong Inferences, Groundless Jealousies and strain'd Constructions: That I shou'd put a very great affront upon your understanding if I supposed it possible you cou'd mean anything in earnest by them; but to put a Stop to my troubling you any more. You have your end Madam, for I will never trouble you more Unless the Duke of Marlborough recovers so far, to shelter me from such intolerable Treatment.

Sir John Vanbrugh to the Duchess of Marlborough, *Correspondence*, 1716

Burleigh House

Westcombe House, Blackheath : One cannot help think-ing soon after one gets into the house that it must have been built by somebody that is mad. Some of the doors in the house are made in what I call a triangle, at least I don't know how to describe it better, but it is ex-tremely fantastical. And one of the rooms which is low-roofed and not much bigger than one of the Duke of Bedford's tables he dines upon when he receives company has four great stone pillars, which I suppose is because the Ancients had pillars to support magnificent large rooms that either wanted or at least appeared to want support. But these pillars take away what little room there is, and are plainly to support nothing. . . .

But the alcoves for the beds to stand in are not less diverting, or they are so ordered that it is not easy to get into them but at the feet of the bed.

There is in the house a vast many wolf's and lion's heads and such sorts of curiosities made, I think, of what they call tobacco pipe clay. And there was one figure I believe my Lady Delawarr would have been mightily pleased with, because the nose was broke off. . . .

Sarah, Duchess of Marlborough, Correspondence, 1732

On the whole the aristocracy adopted a de haut en bas *attitude towards their architects.*

Ld L[ansdowne] seemed highly satisfied tho' sparing in expression & certainly too short. dismissed me with a short audience. invited me to dinner to meet Mr Bowles. Lady L: also short & cold. neither encourage one to familiarity, perhaps rightly.

C. R. Cockerell, Note, 1824

Personality

Men of letters and poets, as well as architectural historians, have left us general descriptions of country houses. In an account of Kalander's house in the Arcadia *Philip Sidney had his own home, Penshurst, in mind. His sentiments were echoed by Ben Jonson a few years later.*

Thou art not, Penshurst, built to envious show
Of touch or marble; nor canst boast a row
Of polish'd pillars or a roofe of gold:
Thou hast no lantherne, whereof tales are told:
Or stayre or courts; but stand'st an ancient pile,
And, these grudg'd at, art reverenc'd the while.
Thou joy'st in better marks, of soile, of ayre,
Of wood, of water: therein thou art faire.
Thou hast thy walkes for health, as well as sport:
Thy Mount, to which the Dryads do resort,
Here Pan and Bacchus their high feastes have made,
Beneath the broad beach and the chestnut shade . . .

And though thy wals be of the countrey stone,
They're rear'd with no man's ruine, no man's
    grone:
There's none that dwell about them wish them
    downe . . .

Ben Jonson, To Penhurst, early 17th century

*Marvell demonstrates a similar disparagement of foreign
exoticism, extolling somewhat puritanically British simplicity and usefulness.*

> Within this sober Frame expect,
> Work of no Forrain *Architect*;
> That unto Caves the Quarries drew,
> And Forrests did to Pastures hew;
> Who of his great design in Pain,
> Did for a Model vault his Brain,
> Whose Columnes should so high be rais'd
> To arch the Brows that on them gaz'd . . .
> What need of all this Marble Crust
> T'impart the wanton Mote of Dust
> That thinks by Breadth the World t'unite
> Though the first Builders fail'd in Height?
> But all things are composed here
> Like Nature, orderly and near . . .

Andrew Marvell, Upon (Nun)Appleton House,
to my Lord Fairfax, 1650

A private and lone house in or neare to Bagley Wood,
between Oxon and Abendon (called Bayworth) is an
old house situated in a romancey place, and a man that
is given to devotion and learning cannot find out a
better place . . . to refresh his mind with a melancholy
walke.

Anthony à Wood, Life & Times, 1659

See, here's the grand approach,
That way is for his grace's coach;
There lies the bridge, and there the clock,
Observe the lion and the cock;
The spacious court, the colonnade,
And mind how wide the hall is made;
The chimneys are so well designed,
They never smoke in any wind:
The galleries contrived for walking,
The windows to retire and talk in;
The council-chamber to debate,
And all the rest are rooms of state.
'Thanks, sir,' cried I, ' 'tis very fine,
But where d'ye sleep, or where d'ye dine?
I find, by all you have been telling,
That 'tis a house, but not a dwelling.'

Jonathan Swift, *Verses on Blenheim*, early 18th century

Chiswick House, Middlesex : Lord Hervey said of the new house at Chiswick, that it was too small to live in, & too big to hang to a Watch.

*

Bleinheim Palace, Oxon : execrable within, without, & almost all round.

*

Chatsworth : The colour of the Stone a soft yellowish brown, enlivened by the gilt bars of the Windows.

Horace Walpole, *Visits to Country Seats*, 1760

Kedleston, Derbs. : Dr Johnson thought better of it today, than when he saw it before; for he had lately attacked it violently, saying, 'It would do excellently for a town-hall. The large room with the pillars (said he) would do for the Judges to sit in at the assizes; the circular room for a jury-chamber; and the rooms above for prisoners.'

[6]

'One should think (said I) that the proprietor of all this must be happy.' 'Nay, Sir (said Johnson), all this excludes but one evil – poverty.'

James Boswell, *Life of Samuel Johnson*, Aug. 1777

Warwick Castle : nothing to disgrace the taste of antiquity, but a vulgar overgrown Roman basin in the centre of the court; which I would toss into the centre of the river, or give to the church for a font.

5th Viscount Torrington, *Diaries*, 1785

The Courtyard, Ightham Mote

Newstead Abbey :
Through thy battlements, Newstead, the hollow winds
    whistle;
  Thou, the hall of my fathers, art gone to decay;
In thy once smiling garden the hemlock and thistle
  Have choked up the rose which late bloomed in
      the way . . .

Shades of heroes, farewell! your descendant departing
  From the seat of his ancestors bids you adieu!
Abroad or at home, your remembrance imparting
  New courage, he'll think upon glory and you.

Though a tear dim his eye at this sad separation,
   'Tis nature, not fear, that excites his regret;
Far distant he goes, with the same emulation,
   The fame of his fathers he ne'er can forget.

That fame and that memory still will he cherish,
   He vows that he ne'er will disgrace your renown;
Like you will he live, or like you will he perish;
   When decayed, may he mingle his dust with your
      own.

           Lord Byron, *On Leaving Newstead Abbey*, 1803

Stoke Farm, near Windsor, Berks : A beautiful ferme
ornée, most comfortable house tho' small; every room
abounds with all that is wanted, luxe more than in
Palaces. A récherche in all things imaginable for use or
agrémens; the best cuisine in Europe, delicious German
baker, Italian office, gardens to vie with Holland for
vegetables, & flowers as good as Haarlem: in short, all
that man or woman can wish for. A shrewd, sensible,
lively, good hearted host [Earl of Sefton] with gay,
lively conversation; & the best natured wife that ever
lived, & cheerful daughters.

           Elizabeth, Lady Holland to her Son, 20.4.1832,
           ed. Earl of Ilchester, 1946

Downton Castle, Herefordshire : I rode to Downton
Castle on Monday, a gimcrack castle and bad house,
built by Payne Knight, an epicurean philosopher, who
after building the castle went and lived in a lodge or
cottage in the park; there he died, not without sus-
picion of having put an end to himself, which would
have been fully conformable to his notions.

           Vol. IV, 26.6.1839

*

Chatsworth, Derbyshire : Chatsworth is very magnificent, but I looked back with regret to the house in its
unfinished state, when we lived in three spacious cheer-

ful rooms looking to the south, which are now quite useless, being gorgeously furnished with velvet and silk, and marble tables, but unoccupied, and the windows closed lest the sun should spoil the finery with which the apartments are decorated. The comfort we had then has been ill exchanged for the magnificence which has replaced it, and the Duke has made the house so large that he cannot afford to live in it, and never remains there above two or three months in the year.

Charles Greville, *Memoirs*, Vol. V, 16.10.1843

Compton Wynyates, Warwickshire : But of Compton Wynyates (the name of this enchanting domicile) I despair of giving any coherent or adequate account. . . . It sits on the grass at the bottom of a wooded hollow, and the glades of a superb old park go wandering upward, away from it. When I came out in front of the house from a short and steep but stately avenue, I said to myself that here surely we had arrived at the farthest limits of what ivy-smothered brick-work and weather-beaten gables, conscious old windows and clustered mossy roofs, can accomplish for the eye. It is impossible to imagine a more perfect picture.

Henry James, *Portraits of Places*, 1877

Knowsley, Derbyshire : This house is enormous and very rambling. There are something over 80 bedrooms, all very small. None of the house is pretty, though some very old, but it has been so patched and pulled about by different owners, especially the last Lord Derby, that it is really hideous. It is built of a dull red brick. The rooms are all small, with the exception of one dining-room which is enormous and a very fine room, only terribly modernized and spoilt. Inside it is very comfortable and nice.

Lady Emily Lutyens, *A Blessed Girl*, 1893

Allington Castle [Kent] and the river all cold and grey and swelling – something evil about its ancientness and turning inward – the windows like eyes that have turned into slots for money – nothing moving along the battlements, only the flag blowing glumly. It should not have been a Union Jack. . . .

Over everything brooded the greed and the joylessness. But it had its own beauty, which was a beauty of mournfulness and lack of understanding. One was not tempted to scrutinize it, to separate the restorations from the ruin, one took it as it was and dumped it down into one's mind as Gloom Castle, Castle Wet, Misery along the river.

Denton Welch, *Journals*, 13.1.1946

Some Famous Inhabitants

English country houses have cradled poets, composers, painters, soldiers, sailors, scientists, explorers, politicians and sportsmen of national and international renown. Their names are almost legion. Furthermore the association of these people with our country houses is often linked with some critical moment of history.

Moseley Old Hall, Staffordshire : In the afternoon reposing himself on the bed in the parlour chamber and inclineing to sleep, as I was watching att the window, one of the soldiers I saw come running in, who told the maid, soldiers were comeing to search, who thereupon presentlie came running to the staires head, and cried, soldiers, soldiers are comeing: which His Majestie [King Charles II] hearing, presentlie started out of his bed, and runn to his privacie where I secured him the best I could, and then leaving him, went forth to meet the soldiers, who were comeing to search, whom as soon as they saw and knew who I was were ready to pull mee in peeces, and take me away with them, saying, I was come from Worcester fight; but after much dispute with them, and by the neighbours being informed of their false information, that I was not there they lett me goe: but till I sawe them clearly all gone forth of the town, I returned not; but as soon as they were I returned to release him, and did acquaint him with my stay, which hee thought long and then he began to bee very chearfull again.

A verbal account by Mr Whitgreave, the owner of Moseley, of his Sovereign's narrow escape while hiding in his house after the Battle of Worcester in 1651. Mr Whitgreave's language is breathless and almost biblical.

§

Houghton Hall, Norfolk : Sir Robert Walpole used always to go into Norfolk twice in a year, for ten days in the summer and twenty in November, and generally set out for his second expedition the day after the King's birthday.

Lord Hervey, *Memoirs*, 1734

At 5 o'clock we set out to Hartwell [Bucks.]. The house is large, but in a dreary, disagreeable situation. The King [Louis XVIII] had completely altered the interior, having sub-divided almost all the apartments in order to lodge a greater number of people. There were numerous outhouses, in some of which small shops had been established by the servants, interspersed with gardens, so that the place resembled a little town. . . .

The King had a manner of swinging his body backwards and forwards, which caused the most unpleasant sensations in that small room, and made my father feel something like being sea-sick. . . . His Majesty did the honours himself, and was very civil and agreeable. We were a very short time at table, and the ladies and gentlemen all got up together. Each of the ladies folded up her napkin, tied it round with a bit of ribbon, and carried it away. After dinner we returned to the drawing-room and drank coffee. . . . Whenever the King came in or went out of the room, Madame d'Angoulême made him a low curtsey, which he returned by bowing and kissing his hand.

Vol. I, 14.4.1814

Holland House, Middlesex : Dined at Holland House. . . . The *tableau* of the house is this:— Before dinner, Lady Holland affecting illness and almost dissolution, but with a very respectable appetite, and after dinner in high force and vigour; Lord Holland, with his chalk-stones and unable to walk, lying on his couch in very good spirits and talking away; [Henry] Luttrell and [Samuel] Rogers walking about, ever and anon looking despairingly at the clock and making short excursions from the drawing room; [John] Allen [the librarian] surly and disputatious, poring over the newspapers. . . . Such is the social despotism of this strange house, which presents an odd mixture of luxury and constraint, of enjoyment physical and intellectual, with an alloy of small *désagréments*. Talleyrand generally comes at ten or eleven o'clock, and stays as long as they will let him.

Though everybody who goes there finds something to abuse or to ridicule in the mistress of the house, or its ways, all continue to go; all like it more or less; and whenever, by the death of either, it shall come to an end, a vacuum will be made in society which nothing will supply. It is the house of all Europe; the world will suffer by the loss; and it may with truth be said that it will 'eclipse the gaiety of nations'.

Charles Greville, Memoirs, Vol. II, 20.11.1832

§

Recollections of J. J. Rousseau's sojourn at Wotton Hall, Staffordshire, where in 1766–7 he took refuge from the consequences of seditious publications in France. He was accompanied by Mademoiselle le Vasseur. At Wotton he wrote most of the Confessions. *William Howitt made a pilgrimage to Wotton to ascertain if any of the local people remembered him.*

'And when,' I asked, 'did this gentleman live here?' 'O' said the man, 'before my time; but there are owd people in the village who were children then, and they remember him. He war mighty curious on yarbs (herbs), and ah've heered see, war skilled to cure welly ony disease wi' em. Owd James Robinson a'th top o'th town, and Farmer Burton here, and owd Missis Saut (Salt), of Ellaston, they know'd him, an' can tell ya au about him.' I walked up and found this James Robinson, a blithe old fellow of about ninety. When I asked if he knew the Frenchman who once lived at the Hall, he replied, 'What, owd Ross Hall? Ay, know him did I, well enough. Ah've seen him monny an' monny a time, every dee welly, coming and going in's comical cap an' ploddy (plaid) gown a'gethering his yarbs.' I asked him if he ever had any talk with him. 'No, he could na speak no English, nubbut a wod or two.' 'And was there anybody here with him?' 'Yes, there war a lady –

they cawd her Madam Zell, but whether how war his wife or not, ah dunna know. Folks said how warna.'

William Howitt, *Visits to Remarkable Places*, Vol. I, 1846

The indefatigable Howitt's researches into the Shakespeare deer-stealing legend in Charlecote Park, Warwickshire were hardly more successful.

It was a fine autumn morning when I set off to walk there [Charlecote], and I pleased myself . . . that I was treading the ground Shakspeare had trod many a time, and gazed on the same scenery, if not on the very identical objects. . . . The woods of Charlecote began to show themselves before me, and presently the house itself, in front of them, stood full in view, and made me exclaim, 'Ay, there is the very place still where Shakspeare encountered the angry old knight in his hall.' . . . As I advanced, I met a country lad; 'So,' I said, 'this, I suppose, is where Shakspeare came for some of Sir Thomas Lucy's deer? You have heard of Shakspeare, I warrant you.' 'Yes,' said the lad, 'often and often, and yonder he is upon a deer that he took.' 'What Shakspeare?' 'Yes, sir, Shakspeare.' I went on towards the image, wondering at the oddity of taste which could induce the Lucys to place an image of Shakspeare there, and with the deer too! When I came near, behold it was a leaden statue of poor innocent Diana. She was in the attitude of the Apollo Belvedere, having apparently just discharged an arrow and watching its career, still holding aloft the bow-hand, and grasping the centre of the bow. Close to her side was the figure of a fallow deer. . . . 'And did you not observe,' I asked, 'that it was a woman, with a woman's bosom, in a woman's dress, and with a crescent on her brow?' 'In troth,' said the man, 'I did na just notice that noo.'

William Howitt, *Visits to Remarkable Places*, Vol. I, 1846

The school room at Chatsworth :

When I think about this room, so many recollections
crowd upon me that I do not know how to begin. In all
the days of my parents' residence here, this room and
the adjoining Breakfast-room were the only habitable
ones they had of a morning, save when, on public days,
or the occasion of some unusual visitors, they resorted
to the apartment on the first floor to the South. Here,
with the door opening to the cold windy passage, they
sat. A plain square green baize-covered table . . . stood
between the fire and the window to the West. Here
Charles Fox, Sheridan, [James] Hare, Lord John
Townshend, Fish Crawford, and many other celeb-
rities conversed; and there was a constant war with
Hare, who did not spare the ladies of the party.

6th Duke of Devonshire, *Handbook to Chatsworth, c.* 1846

A visitor to Hughenden [Manor] found him [Disraeli]
gazing into the fire and murmuring, 'Dreams, dreams,
dreams.'

Reginald, 2nd Viscount Esher, *Cloud Capp'd Towers,* 1927

The Approach

*The first impression of a country house is sometimes
modified but it usually endures. Evelyn, like Pepys and
other visitors to Nonesuch Palace before it was destroyed
in Charles II's reign, was amazed by the painted and
stuccoed panels of the outside walls :*

[I] took an exact view of the plaster statues and bass-
relievos inserted betwixt the timbers and puncheons of
the outside walls of the Court; which must needs have
been the work of some celebrated Italian. I much
admired how they had lasted so well and entire since

the time of Henry VIII, exposed as they are to the air; and pity it is they are not taken out and preserved in some dry place; a gallery would become them. There are some mezzo-relievos as big as the life; the story is of the Heathen Gods, emblems, compartments, etc. . . . I observed that the appearing timber-puncheons, entrelices, etc. were all so covered with scales of slate, that it seemed carved in the wood and painted, the slate fastened on the timber in pretty figures, that has, like a coat of armour, preserved it from rotting.

John Evelyn, *Diary*, 3.1.1666

Ashtead Park, Surrey : all the windows are sarshes and large squares of glass, I observ'd they are double sarshes to make the house the warmer for it stands pretty bleake.

Celia Fiennes, *The Journeys of,* 1698

Holkham, Norfolk : This central front, in every respect that can be named, appears all lightness, elegance and proportion: but when you advance near, you find no entrance to the house; there are no stairs up to the portico; and this circumstance, after so fine an approach, and so long seeing the portico, and expecting it to be the entrance, becomes a disappointment, and is a fault in the building.

*

Blenheim, Oxfordshire : that celebrated palace, which has been by some so excessively abused, and so praised by others. The front is a clutter of parts, so distinct, that a Gothic church has as much unity; and, withal, a heaviness in each part, which is infinitely disgusting . . . . [It is] a quarry, and yet consists of such innumerable and trifling parts, that one would think them the fragments of a rock jumbled together by an earthquake. . . .

Arthur Young, *A Southern Tour,* 1767

Claremont

*The longer the drive the more impressed and awed the
visitor was intended to be, especially if, as in Elizabeth
Bennet's case, she came from a comparatively humble
home :*

They gradually ascended for half-a-mile, and then found
themselves at the top of a considerable eminence,
where the wood ceased, and the eye was instantly
caught by Pemberley House, situated on the opposite
side of a valley, into which the road with some abrupt-
ness wound. It was a large, handsome stone building,
standing well on rising ground, and backed by a ridge
of high woody hills; and in front, a stream of some
natural importance was swelled into greater, but without any artificial appearance. Its banks were neither
formal nor falsely adorned. Elizabeth was delighted.
She had never seen a place for which nature had done
more, or where natural beauty had been so little counter-
acted by an awkward taste. They were all of them
warm in their admiration; and at that moment she felt
that to be mistress of Pemberley might be something!

Jane Austen, *Pride and Prejudice*, 1813

A house in Cambridgeshire:

Some cows lay on the grass just before the door of the house, so that we were obliged almost to ride over them – a strange anomaly, which even Repton animadverts upon. It is the custom here to have the park, that is the ornamented pasture land, extend on one side, if not on both, to the very house; but surely it would be in better taste to have the garden and pleasure-ground around the house. It seems to me that, however agreeable the distant view of cattle may be, their immediate vicinity, with all its accompaniments, is not very pleasant.

Prince Pückler-Muskau, *English Tour,* 19.10.1826

On Entrance

In late Stuart times tapestries and wall-hangings of cotton and damask took the place of oak or painted deal panelling. By the first quarter of the eighteenth century stucco wall frames, often of intricate rococo design, became the general vogue:

Ashtead Park, Surrey: Supped at my Lady Mordaunt's at Ashted, where was a roome hung with pintado [printed East Indian cotton] full of figures great and small, prettily representing sundry trades and occupations of the Indians with their habits.

John Evelyn, *Diary,* 30.11.1665

Newby Hall, Yorkshire: the roomes were mostly wanscoated and painted, the best roome was painted just like marble, few roomes were hung . . . the house is served with water by pipes into a Cistern into the garden cellars and all offices; this was the finest house I saw in Yorkshire.

Celia Fiennes, *The Journeys of,* 1697

Broadlands, Hampshire : The inside, from the Italian taste, strikes me with gloominess, as the height of all the windows is dreadful, and one may judge must be uncomfortably so, as Lady Palmerston has a settee on wheels, which is placed on two or three steps; and on inquiring from the housekeeper what that was for, she replied that her Ladyship might *see* out of the windows. There is a desk on it to read, write, or draw upon, so that the machine is clever, only nowadays, when all windows are down to the ground, one should be more averse to ascend to have a prospect.

Mrs Lybbe Powys, Diaries, 1792

Norbury Park, Surrey : We saw the room which Barrett painted. The Lake scene (an evening) is very ingeniously executed, much superior to the other parts. The whole has a *crowded effect*: but perhaps appeared more so from the room having so many chairs – tables – Harpsichord – Work-baskets, books, etc. – there was scarcely room to move in it – & the pictures on the walls could not be seen but with difficulty.

J. Farington, Diary, 5.7.1803

Knowsley, Lancashire : We all dined at Knowsley last night. The new dining-room is opened: it is 53 feet by 37, and such a height that it destroys the effect of all the other apartments. . . . You enter it from a passage by two great Gothic church-like doors the whole height of the room. This entrance is in itself fatal to the effect. Ly Derby (like herself), when I objected to the immensity of the doors, said: 'You've heard Genl. Grosvenor's remark upon them have you not? He asked in his grave, pompous manner – "Pray are those great doors to be opened for every pat of butter that comes into the room?" ' At the opposite end of the room is an immense Gothic window, and the rest of the light is given by a sky-light mountains high. There

[19]

are two fireplaces; and the day we dined there, there were 36 wax candles over the table, 14 on it, and ten great lamps on tall pedestals about the room; and yet those at the bottom of the table said it was quite petrifying in that neighbourhood, and the report here is that they have since been obliged to abandon it entirely from the cold.

Vol. II, 15.12.1822

✻

Raby Castle, Durham : This house is itself *by far* the most magnificent and unique in several ways that I have ever seen. . . . As long as I have heard of anything, I have heard of being driven into the hall of this house in one's carriage, and being set down by the fire. You can have no idea of the magnificent perfection with which this is accomplished. Then the band of musick which plays in this same hall during dinner! then the gold plate!! and then – the poplolly [his hostess, Lady Darlington] at the head of all!!!

Thomas Creevey, *Papers*, Vol. II, 16.2.1825

Here is a mid-Victorian novelist belonging to a robust age who reacts from the flimsiness of old-fashioned Georgian furnishings :

Dorothea . . . found the house and grounds all that she could wish; the dark bookshelves in the long library, the carpets and curtains with colours subdued by time, the curious old maps and bird's-eye views on the walls of the corridor, with here and there an old vase below, had no oppression for her, and seemed more cheerful than the casts and pictures at the Grange, which her uncle had long ago brought home from his travels. . . .

'Oh Dodo,' said Celia, 'will you not have the bow-windowed room upstairs?'

Mr Casaubon led the way thither. The bow-window looked down the avenue of limes; the furniture was all

of a faded blue, and there were miniatures of ladies
and gentlemen with powdered hair hanging in a group.
A piece of tapestry over a door also showed a blue-
green world with a pale stage in it. The chairs and
tables were thin-legged and easy to upset. It was a
room where one might fancy the ghost of a tight-laced
lady revisiting the scene of her embroidery. A light
book-case contained duodecimo volumes of polite
literature in calf, completing the furniture.

George Eliot, *Middlemarch*, Bk. I, ch. ix., 1871-2

*Harold Nicolson recorded nostalgic childhood memories
of entering his uncle, Lord Dufferin's house, Clandeboye
in County Down:*

First would come the scrape of wood on stone, since
the door was continued downwards by a hinged flap
or flange which protected the hall from the draughts
of northern Ireland and which would rise as the door
was opened, scraping upwards along the step. Then
would come a puff of inside air, the smell of the outer
hall (a smell of stone and plaster), the fainter smell of
the inner hall (a smell of varnished deal and velvet

cushions) and thereafter a mingled foretaste of all the other smells of that large house, from the smell of grapes and marsala in the dining-room, to the smell of French polish in the saloon, the smell of calf bindings in the library, the smell of dried rose leaves and picture varnish in the great gallery, the smell of sandal-wood which spread outwards from the Pompeian cup-boards of my aunt's dressing-room.

Harold Nicolson, *Helen's Tower*, 1937

It was an aesthetic education to live within those walls, to wander from room to room, from the Soanesque library to the Chinese drawing-room, adazzle with gilt pagodas and nodding mandarins, painted paper and Chippendale fretwork, from the Pompeian parlour to the great tapestry-hung hall which stood unchanged, as it had been designed 250 years before; to sit, hour after hour, in the pillared shade looking out on the terrace.

Evelyn Waugh, *Brideshead Revisited*, 1945

Pictures and Furniture

Curiosities had more appeal for the average seventeenth-century visitor than works of art. Gradually under-standing and appreciation of the latter improved.

Swakeleys, Middlesex : Pretty to see over the skreene of the hall . . . the King's head, and my Lord of Essex on one side, and Fairfax on the other; and upon the other side of the skreene, the parson of the parish, and the lord of the manor and his sisters. [Sir R. Viner] showed me a black boy that he had, that died of a consumption, and being dead, he caused him to be dried in an oven, and lies there entire in a box.

Samuel Pepys, *Diary*, 7.9.1665

Burghley House, Northants : Very fine paint in pictures, but they were all without garments, or very little, that was the only fault, the immodesty of the pictures, especially in my Lord's apartment.

Celia Fiennes, *Journeys of,* 1697

The carpet in our drawing room covers all the floor and has done so perhaps for many years, as its threadbare state witnesseth. Uninterrupted, then, and unmolested are all the fleas and other small nations who therein inhabit. . . . Let Dan Martin therefore take up this carpet; let it be turned out upon the lawn so soon as this rainy weather has given place to sunshine and dryness. There let it be shook and beat without mercy by the strong hands of both gardeners. During its absence let the floor, whose dirt it has so long concealed, be finally and totally rid of said dirt by means of a good scouring. . . . But you will recommend doubtless some able-bodied matron, honest and not pregnant, who will scour this floor once and again till it becomes perfectly clean; after which it may be dry-rubbed by the gardener's wife, using her husband's arms, that is teaching him how to dry-rub a room.

Fanny Boscawen, *Correspondence,* 27.6.1787

Coleorton, Leicestershire : Till one o Clock I was employed on my drawings, and then rode with Sir George [Beaumont] to Charlewood Forest abt. 3 miles distant to see some picturesque rocks. On our way He told me that He should have been much inclined to leave His collection of pictures to the public were there a proper place to deposit them in either at the British Museum or the Royal Academy. He foresaw the impossibility of preserving them for any great length of time in a family at least witht. a probability of there being much injury done to them by injudicious cleaning of them by ignorant persons, as had been the case at Hooker in

Lancashire (Lord George Cavendish's) and other places, so that at present there are very few pictures by Claude in perfect preservation: the other reason was that from temporary want of money to pay debts or portion Children it might be found convenient to part with such property and the collection would then become scattered.

J. Farington, *Diary*, Vol. VII, 16.10.1812

Littlecote, Wiltshire : King William III slept at Littlecote for two or three nights in 1689 . . . and he seems to have left behind him a good many papers, which have ever since been preserved in the house. There is also a large collection of miscellaneous letters of the time of the Civil War, more or less curious, which were preserved by a lucky accident. Popham told me that his father told him there was a mass of papers in an old box under the roof of the house which had better be destroyed. His son went up for the purpose, and discovered the contents of the box, saved the papers, and had them arranged in a book. [*Among these papers was the correspondence of Queen Henrietta Maria with Charles I when she went to Holland.*]

Charles Greville, *Memoirs*, Vol. VIII, 11.5.1858

Chatsworth, Derbs : The late Mrs Strong, my distinguished predecessor [as Librarian] told me on her last visit to Chatsworth that one of her duties had been to tour the principal rooms with the 8th Duke and his [German] Duchess [of Devonshire] the day before a house-party began, and tell them a few outstanding facts about their principal possessions. In [the China Closet] hangs a very important picture . . . for it bears the signature of Jan Van Eyck and the date 1421. The subject is the enthronement of an archbishop – traditionally identified as St Thomas Becket, but now known to be St Romold. . . . The Saint is represented seated on his throne and, following the convention of the period, the Dove hovers above his head. On one of these tours . . . Mrs Strong was beginning her patter about this picture when the Duchess interrupted in her woolly guttural – 'What's that extraordinary bird that's got into the Cathedral?' This was an opportunity for His Grace to display his learning. 'Why,' he murmured into his beard, 'even I knew that was the Holy Ghost.'

Francis Thompson, *A History of Chatsworth*, 1949

Libraries and Books

It is fairly safe to say that before Tudor times no books were to be found in castles or country houses. In spite of the renaissance of learning under Henry VIII,

Many country houses still had no books at all. . . . Many gentlemen, especially in the remoter parts of the country, still preferred to hawk and hunt; in Northumberland, in the 1560s, ninety-two out of the 146 leading gentry were unable to sign their name. In 1601 Bess of Hardwick . . . only had six books at Hardwick, kept in her bedchamber. Sir William Fairfax, who installed the magnificent great chamber at Gilling Castle, owned thirty-nine books. Only a dozen or so members of the upper classes (exclusive of clerics) are known to have owned more than a hundred books in the sixteenth century. . . . Only two great men – Lord Lumley and Lord Burghley – owned more than a thousand books.

Mark Girouard, *Life in the English Country House*, 1978

My Lord [Tyrconnel] has a well furnished library here [Belton House]; in order to fill up the vacant spaces on the shelves he has invented titles for books that are carved in wood, as Standstill's *Travels*, Block's

[25]

Thoughts, Short Proceedings in Chancery, Dennis on the *Dunciad*, etc.

Philip Yorke, Travel Journal of, 1744

Luton Hoo, Beds : 'This is one of the places I do not regret having come to see. . . . The Library is very splendid.'

Samuel Johnson in Boswell's Life, 1781

Felbrigg, Norfolk : The Library is upstairs, and in a room adjoining to it Mr Windham [William, the statesman] always sat when engaged in business or study. When He was last at Felbrigg, which was in the autumn of 1809 He was alone there for about 8 weeks, and had only a few of His family connexions to call upon him. During this time he slept in a small tent bed put up in a niche in a room, next to His sitting room, for the convenience of it being near the Library. An Old Maid Servant who shewed us the House gave these and many other particulars respecting Him. She said she has gone into the Library at Six o Clock in the morning & has found Him there engaged in reading, and that He wd afterwards return to His bed as His usual time of rising was abt. 8 o Clock & He breakfasted about nine.

J. Farington, Diary, Vol. VII, 1812

I wish you could see my library here [West Moulsey, Berks]. I think it a model for a book-drawing-room; it is but just finished, and all in the very cheapest way; but every one who has seen or sat in it are delighted with it. It is rather odd, and would frighten poor Smirke [the architect] by its angles and irregularities; but it is warm and comfortable, and holds 3000 volumes without diminishing the size of the room, and without having, I think, any of the sombre formality of a library. I have besides a little den which holds 1000 volumes more, and in which I *work*. In short, with the drawbacks which I have mentioned, I am as happy in my mind, as satisfied with my very moderate fortunes, and as contented with my humble location and still humbler avocations as it is possible to be.

J. W. Croker, *Papers*. Letter to Sir Robert Peel, 15.11.1832

I went on Monday to Althorp, and was very well amused among the pictures and books, though as there are 50,000 volumes of the latter, it was only possible to look at the outside of them, and here and there examine some remarkable book or fine edition. They are kept in admirable condition, and the present Lord, without being a bibliomaniac like his father, keeps the collection up, and buys from time to time anything in the market that may be necessary to complete it.

Charles Greville, *Memoirs*, 15.3.1845

Indeed the father, the 2nd Earl Spencer, was one of the greatest book collectors of all time.

Music

*Masques, accompanied by music and dancing, were popular
in Elizabeth I's reign. They reached a climax of favour
with the court of Charles I under the production of Inigo
Jones. But by the turn of the seventeenth century any
excuse for having music on special occasions in a country
house was seized upon. Professional musicians did not
however rank very high in the social scale.*

At great feasts, when the Earl's service is going to the
table, they are to play upon Shagbutte, Cornets,
Shalms and such other instruments giving with wind.
In meal times to play upon Viols, Violins, or other
broken music. They are to teach the Earl's children to
sing and play upon the Base Viol, the Virginals, Lute,
Bandera or Cittern. In some houses they are allowed
a mess of wheat in their chambers, in other houses they
eat with the waiters.

R.B., *Some Rules and Orders for the Government of the House
of an Earle, c.* 1605 (Quoted in M. Girouard, *Life in the
English Country House,* 1978)

*During the eighteenth and nineteenth centuries families in
distant and remote country houses like the Cornewalls at
Moccas Court on the Welsh Marches entertained themselves and their close neighbours with improvised concerts.*

My mother was very fond of music & encouraged all
[her daughters'] musical tastes. Cumador was their
master for song, also Viganni, a tenor on the operatic
stage, used to come to Moccas, & Dragonetti the
wonderful double bass player, also Sh—, a beautiful
violinist, & of course they had several amateur friends
who used to come to Moccas in the summer (in those
days no one wished to attempt the roads in winter).
Then your father came home from abroad, The Grand

[28]

Tour about 1797 I should guess, with his violoncello, & later my younger brother, Charles, played on the violin. Harriet sang very nicely but not like her two sisters. They all worked hard inventing a kind of score of Mozart's & Haydn's pieces, so that the organ (which I only blew for them) & the piano forte could fill up the Haut Boys & other wind instrumental parts.

In these days the Piano Forte was sacred from vulgar fingers & I practised on the Harpsicord for many years. . . . In these days it was customary for people to sing at the Dessert table, & Fanny sang delightfully, Ballads, 'The Thorn', 'Crazy Jane', 'The Orphan's Prayer', till tears rolled down people's cheeks listening to her. Some gentlemen came to Moccas and they too sang after dinner, Captain Morris, Colonel Scudamore, etc., etc., and my sisters and they sang catches & glees at table without accompaniment.

> Lady Duff Gordon (née Caroline Cornewall) to her niece,
> Mrs A. C. Master (unpubl.), 20.11.1872

Wheatley, Yorks: This was the country seat of Sir Bryan Cook, where every fortnight I used to spend two or three days. Sir Bryan played the violin and some of his relations generally came from Doncaster to make up morning concerts. Our music was chiefly Corelli, Geminiani, etc. Lady Cook loved music and I gave her lessons on the guitar, which was then a fashionable instrument.

> Sir William Herschel, *Memorandum*, 1.1.1766

Privies and Baths

Until the last half of the eighteenth century sanitation in country houses was extremely elementary. It remained fairly unsatisfactory until the end of the nineteenth century.

Longford Castle, Wilts: Nay, art here hath so well traced Nature in the most ignoble conveyances (which are no less needful than the most visible conveniences) as to furnish every storey with private conduits for the suillage of the house, which are washed by every shower that falls from the gutters, and so hath vent from the very foundations to the top for the discharge of noisome vapours, by a contrivance not enough followed elsewhere in England, tho' recommended by Architects.

Pelate, *A Longford Manuscript*, 1678

Chatsworth, Derbs: there is a fine grottoe all stone pavement roofe and sides, this is design'd to supply all the house with water besides severall fancyes to make diversion; within this is a batheing roome, the walls all with blew and white marble the pavement mix'd one stone white another black another of the red rance marble; the bath is one entire marble all white finely veined with blew and is made smooth, but had it been as finely pollish'd as some, it would have been the finest marble that could be seen; it was as deep as one's middle on the outside and you went down steps into the bath big enough for two people; at the upper end are two Cocks to let in one hott the other cold water to attemper it as persons please; the windows are all private [i.e. ground] glass.

Celia Fiennes, *The Journeys of*, 1697

Wentworth Woodhouse, Yorks: There is a little skittle ground for the youth to divert them selves, not to omit a beautiful temple to Cloacina with a portico round it, supported by columns made of the natural trunks of trees.

Richard Pococke, *Journey into England*, 1750

Woburn Abbey, Beds: Men's time at day's work for His Grace the Duke of Bedford from November 15th to the

22nd, 1760 To squarring and setting Dutch tiles in His Grace's water closet in the garden.

Woburn Abbey Accounts, 1760

I breakfasted the day before yesterday at Aelia Laelia Chudleigh's . . . of all curiosities, are the *Conveniences* in every bedchamber; great mahogany projections, as big as her own bubbies, with the holes, with brass handles, and cocks, etc. I could not help saying it was the *loosest* family I ever saw! Never was such an intimate union of love and a closestool! Adieu!

Horace Walpole to George Montagu, 27.3.1760

Elizabeth, 1st Duchess of Northumberland was deliciously candid about the sanitary arrangements, or the lack of them, in the various grand country houses she visited during the age of elegance.

At Hopetoun House : The housekeeper sent me into the Closet to look for a Chamber pot but it being in a Box I could not find it.

Elizabeth, 1st Duchess of Northumberland,
Travel Journals (unpubl.), 1771

But at Harewood she was only too easily directed to 'a water closet which stinks all over the house'.

As for personal cleanliness before the days of hip baths and running water even Dukes were often grubby.

The numerous visitors to Moccas included :

the old Duke of Norfolk (in his old coach and 4 black horses) who always drank like a fish, & it was said that he used to make a compromise with his coachman, saying, 'John, you must be sober tonight, I shall be drunk,' or vice versa. Sometimes he slept at Moccas, but never brought a clean shirt with him & came down to breakfast next morning with a portwine spotted shirt, generally himself unwashed. The servants considered him a *dear* man, as he never wanted any water in his bedroom.

Lady Duff Gordon to her niece,
Mrs A. C. Master (unpubl.), 20.11.1872

With the arrival of the Edwardian age sybaritism had taken the place of asceticism in plumbing.

People were called by their valets at eight-thirty. These silent but hostile men would arrive bearing in their left hand a neat brass can of shaving water, and in their right hand a neat brass tray of tea, toast, and Marie biscuits. The Edwardian, blinking plethoric eyes above his pink silk eiderdown, would munch the biscuits and would sip the tea. He would then adjust his teeth, adjust his hair, adjust his Afghan dressing-robe, and slouch plethoric along the passage to the bathroom. If he were staying in a rich house (and all houses in the Edwardian epoch were rich), he would find in the bathroom the scented smell of his predecessor's indulgence, the half-empty bottles ('flacons' was the word they used) which contained Hammam Bouquet of Mr Penthalicon. The guest would pour this unguent into the bath, from which his valet would already have removed the stains, the soap-suds and the other *disjecta membra* of the former occupant. The water would be tepid. Edwardian water was always tepid. His predecessor had left his signet-ring in the soap-dish. Through the smell of Hammam Bouquet would gradually pierce the smell of lavender bags and Sanitas. Disgusted and dyspeptic, the Edwardian would proceed with his bath. He shaved in it.

Harold Nicolson, *The Edwardian Weekend* (from *Small Talk*), 1937

Cold and Heating

Until quite recently by far the worst rigour of the English country house was the cold. And the larger the house the colder. In the mid-eighteenth century the rich would buy stoves in Paris.

Woburn Abbey: 'Je reconnois avoir reçue de Milady Comtesse de Bath, par les mains de Milady Lambert, la somme de six cent quarante quatre livres huit sols neuf deniers pour le montant de cinq poêles de fayence y compris fraix de Paris à Rouen et abord du vaisseau dont je donne une double quittance pour ne servir que d'une seulle et même à Paris, le 30 mars, 1756. ENDERLIN.

Receipt for 5 faience stoves from Paris to Woburn

Bramshill, Hampshire: Went to dine at Sir John Cope's, in Hampshire, a most immense pile of building . . . . The range of apartments are so vastly spacious that one generally sees Sir John toward the winter put on his hat to go from one room to another.

October 1766

*

Hardwicke Court, Oxfordshire: The intense cold all January was hardly bearable. I could do nothing but read, was forced to keep warm gloves on, and never quitted the fireside when indoors, tho' made it a rule to walk every day when the snow was not falling. People were sadly alarmed about firing, as the coals at

[33]

Reading and Henley were just gone, and vessels could not get up with more. We thought ourselves particularly fortunate that our London stock lasted till the last week, when we got half a sack from Henley, of such terrible sweepings up that they were really of little use, and no wood to be got.

Mrs Lybbe Powys, *Diaries*, 2.2.1795

Hatfield House, Herts: The whole house, including kitchen and wash-house is heated by one steam-engine.

Prince Pückler-Muskau, *English Tour*, 1826–8

Hesleyside, Northumberland: Coal and firewood they had in great abundance, it is true, but the long passages had no heat, the outside doors were never shut, the hall and corridors were paved with flagstones, while to complete the resemblance of Hesleyside to a refrigerator, the grand staircase, also of stone, and the three large, old-fashioned full-length windows, half way up with the frames warped by the excessive damp, the pride of Mrs [Fenwick] Charlton's heart, continued to make the downstairs space a cave of icy blasts. Even in my early years at Hesleyside funguses grew on the passage woodwork. The dining-room . . . did not have window curtains until some little time after my arrival in 1839.

Barbara Charlton, *Recollections of a Northumbrian Lady*, 1815–66

Superstition and the Eerie

Evidently Fanny Boscawen, that matter-of-fact lady, pooh-poohed a superstition which certainly holds good today.

Badminton, Glos: We are quite alone, and therefore

sit down only thirteen at dinner, but we have had company until yesterday.

Fanny Boscawen, *Correspondence*, 9.9.1791

Ampthill House, Bedfordshire : We have delayed our departure to the 9th. 8th, being Friday, was impossible.
Elizabeth, Lady Holland to her Son, 6.9.1826

The apparition of a Radiant Boy and the incident of a screaming skull are common to several country houses. A clergyman of the Church of England recorded his and his wife's experience at Corby Castle, Cumberland, 163 years ago :

'Soon after we went to bed we fell asleep: it might be between one and two in the morning when I awoke. I observed that the fire was totally extinguished; but although that was the case, and we had no light, I saw a glimmer in the centre of the room, which suddenly increased to a bright flame. I looked out, apprehending that something had caught fire; when, to my amazement, I beheld a beautiful boy, clothed in white, with bright locks resembling gold, standing by my bedside, in which position he remained some minutes, fixing his eyes upon me with a mild and benevolent expression. He then glided gently towards the side of the chimney, where it is obvious there is no possible egress, and entirely disappeared. I found myself again in total darkness, and all remained quiet until the usual hour of rising. I declare this to be a true account of what I saw at Corby Castle upon my word as a clergyman. Henry A ... Rector of Greystoke, 22 Dec. 1824.'
John Ingram, *Haunted Houses*, 1911

When I stayed – in 1936 – at Bradshaw Hall near Bolton there were two skulls mounted on silver seventeenth-century stems. They were religiously kept upon a Family Bible. Colonel Hardcastle, the owner,

[35]

told me that one day his housemaid in dusting broke a skull off its stem. He took both skull and stem to the local jeweller's to be mended. But that night and the following such a caterwauling ensued from the skull left behind in the house that he and the servants were terrified. Colonel Hardcastle had to retrieve the broken skull and stem, and beg the jeweller to come and mend them in the room to which they belonged. He never had any further trouble. One of the skulls was supposed to be Bradshaw the regicide's, and the other his wife's.

J. L-M, *Ancestral Voices*, 1975

Gardens and Parks

Before they became landscape gardeners the English were botanists. In the sixteenth century they imported exotic plants from overseas.

It is a world to see how many strange herbs, plants and unusual fruits are daily brought unto us from the Indies, Americas, Taprobane, Canary Isles and all parts of the world.

William Harrison, *Description of England*, 1577

Beddington, Surrey : famous for the first orange garden in England, being now overgrown trees, planted in the ground, and secured in winter with a wooden tabernacle and stoves. . . . The pomegranates bear here.

John Evelyn, *Diary*, 27.9.1658

A garden remote or by itself is neither pleasant nor useful. Therefore, wherever your house is, near it must be your garden.

John Worlidge, *Systema Horticulturae*, 1677

The tools are to be carried into the Tool-house, and other instruments set in their places, every night when you leave work; and in wet weather you are to cleanse, sharpen and repair them.

John Evelyn, *Directions for his Gardener*, 1687

Chatsworth, Derbyshire : There is another green walke and about the middle of it by the grove stands a fine willow tree, the leaves, barke and all looks very naturall, the roote is full of rubbish or great stones to appearance and all on a sudden by turning a sluce it raines from each leafe and from the branches like a shower, it being made of brass and pipes to each leafe, but in appearance is exactly like any willow. Beyond this is a bason in which are the branches of two hartichocks leaves which weeps at the end of each leafe into the bason which is placed at the foote of lead steps 30 in number.

Celia Fiennes, *The Journeys of*, 1696

Villa at Twickenham

Water jokes were horribly popular throughout Europe in the seventeenth century. The Chatsworth willow-tree has miraculously survived. Topiary assumed astonishing and often grotesque features :

[37]

Adam and Eve in yew; Adam a little shattered by the fall of the Tree of Knowledge in the great storm. Eve and the Serpent very flourishing. . . . A quickset Hog shot up into a Porcupine, by being forgot a week in rainy weather. . . . A Lavender Pigg with Sage growing in his belly.

Alexander Pope, *On Gardening*, Essay in the *Guardian*, 29.9.1713

Goodwood Park, Sussex : But this place is most famous for a great variety of forest trees and shrubs; they have thirty different kinds of oak, and four hundred different American trees and shrubs, which compose one wilderness.

*

Painshill, Surrey : A narrow walk leads . . . over the river, which conducts to a wheel for raising water, an invention of Mr Hamilton's; it consists of four spiral square pipes from the radius to the center, the mouth being open; it conveys the water to the axel where 'tis emptied, and the water is convey'd by pipes to the piece of water I have mentioned.

*

Wroxton Abbey, Oxon : We then descended to a serpentine river, which is supplyed from the large pieces of water; and going up by it we came to the Gothic open rotundo of Mr Miller's design, in which he has practis'd curtains, that by turning screws let down so as to afford shelter which every way you please.

Richard Pococke, *Travels Through England*, 1754, 1756

Artificial ruins required much nicety of composition.
' . . . ruins, my Lord! and they are reckoned very fine ones too. You would think them ready to tumble on your head. It has just cost me a hundred and fifty pounds, to put my ruins in thorough repair.'

Mrs Sterling in Colman and Garrick's
The Clandestine Marriage, 1766

Stourhead, Wiltshire : I have seen the most celebrated gardens in England but these far exceed them all. Others were delighted with the temples, but I was not (1) because several of the statues about them were mean; (2) because I cannot admire the images of devils – and we know the gods of the heathen are but devils; (3) because I defy all mankind to reconcile statues with nudities either to common sense or common decency.

J. Wesley, *Journal*, 12.9.1776

Rough, uncultivated ground, dismal to the eye, inspires peevishness and discontent; may this not be one cause of the harsh manner of savages?

Lord Kames, *The Gentleman Farmer*, 1776

Luton Hoo, Bedfordshire : Dr Johnson made two or three peculiar observations; as when shewn the botanical garden, 'Is not every garden a botanical garden?'

James Boswell, *Life of Samuel Johnson*, 1781

'You have a very small park here,' returned Lady Catherine, after a short silence.

'It is nothing in comparison of Rosings, my Lady, I dare say; but, I assure you, it is much larger than Sir William Lucas's,' [Mrs Bennet answered]. . . .

'Miss Bennet, there seemed to be a prettyish kind of a little wilderness on one side of your lawn. I should be glad to take a turn in it, if you will favour me with your company.'

'Go, my dear,' cried her mother, 'and show her Ladyship about the different walks. I think she will be pleased with the hermitage.'

Lady Catherine de Bourgh in *Pride and Prejudice*, 1813

Sandleford Priory, Berks : Came through a place called 'a park' belonging to a Mr Montagu, who is now abroad. . . . Of all the ridiculous things I ever saw in my life this place is the most ridiculous. The house looks like a sort of church. . . . There is a sort of swamp, at the foot of a wood, at no great distance from the front of the house. . . . Here is the *grand en petit*, or mock magnificence, more complete than I ever beheld it before. Here is a *fountain*, the basin of which is not four feet over, and the water spout not exceeding the pour from a tea-pot. Here is a *bridge* over a *river* of which a child four years old would clear the banks at a jump. . . . In short, such fooleries I never before beheld; but what I disliked most was the apparent impiety of a part of these works of refined taste.

William Cobbett, *Rural Rides*, 30.10.1821

Improvements

On the outbreak of the Civil War John Evelyn in great distress retired from London to his ancestral home of Wotton, Surrey:

I returned, with no little regret, for the confusion that threatened us. Resolving to possess myself in some quiet, if it might be, in a time of so great jealousy, I built by my brother's permission a study, made a fish-pond, an island, and some other solitudes and retirements at Wotton; which gave the first occasion of improving them to those water-works and gardens which afterwards succeeded them, and became at that time the most famous of England.

John Evelyn, *Diary*, 2.5.1643

The poet, Alexander Pope, was among the first to inveigh against what he called

the false taste of magnificence; the first grand error of which is to imagine that 'greatness' consists in the 'size' and 'dimension', instead of the 'proportion' and 'harmony' of the 'whole', and the second, either in joining together 'parts incoherent', or too 'minutely resembling', or in the 'repetition' of the 'same' too frequently.

In other words he deprecated too much formality and pretension in landscape garden layout :—

> To build, to plant whatever you intend,
> To rear the column, or the arch to bend,
> To swell the terrace, or to sink the grot;
> In all, let Nature never be forgot.
> But treat the goddess like a modest fair,
> Nor over-dress, nor leave her wholly bare;
> Let not each beauty everywhere be spied,
> Where half the skill is decently to hide.
> He gains all points who pleasingly confounds,
> Surprises, varies, and conceals the bounds.
>
> Alexander Pope, *Epistle to Lord Burlington*, 1733–4

Fashion necessarily dictated frequent changes of method in landscape gardening. But never so drastically as when the Picturesque school swept away the formality of previous ages. Capability Brown was the leading practitioner of the Picturesque layout in the last half of the eighteenth century.

> He speaks. The lake in front becomes a lawn.
> Woods vanish, hills subside, and vallies rise:
> And streams, as if created for his use
> Pursue the track of his directing wand,
> Sinuous or straight, now rapid and now slow,
> Now murm'ring soft, now roaring in cascades –
> E'en as he bids! Th'enraptur'd owner smiles.
>
> William Cowper, *The Task : The Garden*, 1784

Novelists made mock of the pretensions of the improvers to put all nature in a strait-jacket; Jane Austen, for example, on Mr Crawford's proposals for Thornton Lacey,

*and Thomas Love Peacock in a celebrated piece of satire
upon Payne Knight:*

Immediately after his arrival at Headlong Hall, Mr
Milestone 'a picturesque landscape gardener of the
first celebrity,' showed himself 'impatient to take a
walk round the grounds, that he might examine how
far the system of clumping and levelling could be
carried advantageously into effect.' After he had walked
a few paces, 'I perceive,' said Mr Milestone, 'these
grounds have never been touched by the finger of
taste. . . . My dear Sir, accord me your permission to
wave the wand of enchantment over your grounds.
The rocks shall be blown up, the trees shall be cut
down, the wilderness and all its goats shall vanish
like mist. Pagodas and Chinese bridges, gravel walks
and shrubberies, bowling-greens, canals and clumps
of larch shall rise upon its ruins.'

Before long, Mr Milestone had produced his port-
folio in order to point out the beauties of his plans for
Lord Littlebrain's park, and the following conversation
ensued:

'*Mr Milestone.* This, you perceive, is the natural
state of one part of the grounds. Here is a wood . . .

[42]

thick, intricate and gloomy. Here is a little stream, dashing from stone to stone, and overshadowed by these untrimmed boughs.

'*Miss Tenorina*. The sweet romantic spot!

'*Miss Graziosa*. Dear sister! how can you endure the horrid thicket?

'*Mr Milestone*. You are right, Miss Graziosa: your taste is correct – perfectly *en règle*. Now here is the same place corrected – trimmed – polished – decorated – adorned. Here sweeps a plantation, in that beautiful regular curve: there winds a gravel walk: here are parts of the old wood, left in these majestic circular clumps, disposed at equal distances with wonderful symmetry . . . here is another part of the grounds in its natural state; here is a large rock, with the mountain ash rooted in its fissures, overgrown, as you see, with ivy and moss; and from this part of it bursts a little fountain, that runs bubbling down its rugged sides.

'*Miss Tenorina*. Oh how beautiful! How I should love the melody of that miniature cascade!

'*Mr Milestone*. Beautiful, Miss Tenorina! Base, common and popular. . . . Now observe the meta-morphosis; here is the same rock, cut into the shape of a giant; in one hand he holds a horn, through which that little fountain is thrown to a prodigious elevation. In the other is a ponderous stone, so exactly balanced as to be apparently ready to fall on the head of any person who may happen to be beneath; and there is Lord Littlebrain walking under it.'

Thomas Love Peacock, *Headlong Hall*, 1816

And so it continues.

§

The trouble with the Early Victorians was that they could not leave well alone. Of all the Lucys who had lived at Charlecote Park century after century George and his wife Mary Elizabeth most venerated the Tudor house

[43]

*of their ancestors and its association with Shakespeare.
Yet between 1823 and 1867 they totally obliterated its
antiquity by extensive alterations and 're-edifications'.*

He allowed his wife to root up the untidy plots in the
court and replace them with a fair imitation of an
Elizabethan knot garden. Less happily . . . he removed
the organ gallery and the Tudor screen from the Great
Hall and put a light oak dado round it. More unhappily
still, he allowed Willement, on whose judgement he
had come to depend, to flatten the ceiling of the hall
(the Elizabethan gallery that ran the length of the top
storey had been divided up into servants' attics).
Willement's heavy barrel vaulting with its outsize
Tudor roses robs the hall of impressiveness. Never
for a moment did the Lucys lose sight of Tudor England; even the door handles were carved with Tudor
roses. Twisted pseudo-Jacobean chimnies gave the
roof the richly fretted and pinnacled outline which our
great-grandparents so much admired.

Alice Fairfax-Lucy, *Charlecote and the Lucys*, 1958

Taste, Good and Bad

*As in gardens and parks so in houses taste fluctuated
throughout the centuries. Few people would agree today
with the following diatribe on the surroundings of
Chatsworth:*

A country so deform'd, the traveller
Would swear those parts nature's pudenda were.

Charles Cotton, *The Wonders of the Peak*, 1681

Chinese taste – the principals are a good choice of
chains and bells, and different colours of paint. As to
the serpents, dragons, and monkeys, etc., they, like
the rest of the beauties, may be cut in paper and pasted

[44]

on anywhere, or in any manner. A few laths, nailed across each other, and made black, red, blue, yellow, or any other colour, or mixed with any sort of chequer work, or impropriety of ornament, completes the whole.

R. Morris, *Architectural Remembrancer*, 1751

Lord Brooke . . . has sash'd the great Apartment [at Warwick Castle] and being since told that square sash-windows were not Gothic, he has put certain whim-whams within side the glass, which appearing through, are to look like fretwork. Then he has scooped out a little burrough in the massy walls of the place for his little self and his children which is hung with chintzes in the exact manner of Berkeley Square or Argyle Buildings. What in short can a Lord do nowadays that is lost in a great old solitary castle but skulk about and get into the first hole he finds, as a rat would do in like case?

Thomas Gray to P. Wharton, *Correspondence*, 18.9.1754

Hardwick Hall, Derbyshire : Vast rooms, no taste. Much indifferent tapestry.

*

Clandon Park, Surrey : rather wanting taste than in a bad one.

Horace Walpole, *Visits to Country Seats*, 1764

Vanbrugh, whose buildings are monuments of the vilest taste.

Arthur Young, *A Southern Tour*, 1767

Sion House, Middlesex : Mr Adam has published the first number of his *Architecture*. In it is a magnificent gateway and screen for the Duke of Northumberland at Sion, which I see erecting every time I pass. It is all lace and embroidery, and as *croquant* as his frames for tables; consequently most improper to be exposed in

the high-road to Brentford. From Kent's mahogany
we are dwindled to Adam's filigree. Grandeur and
simplicity are not yet in fashion. . . . Wyatt has employed the antique with more judgement, and the
Pantheon is still the most beautiful edifice in England.
What are the Adelphi buildings? warehouses laced
down the seams, like a soldier's trull in a regimental
old coat.

> Horace Walpole to Revd William Mason,
> *Correspondence*, 29.7.1773

Castle Howard, Yorkshire : I was infinitely struck &
surprised with the first view of Castle Howard from
the new road, which is like a Terrass opposite to it.
The ingredients compose the grandest scene of real
magnificence I ever saw. . . . The house, tho' the Style
is bad, is far superior to Blenheim & has little of its
ponderosity.

> Horace Walpole, *Visits to Country Seats*, 1772

Powderham Castle, Devon : When we got there we found
it not worth a halfpenny.

> William Gilpin, *Observations on
> Western Parts of England*, 1798

Wilton, Wiltshire : Merely to *see*, 'tis certainly one of
the finest sights in England; but to reside at, 'tis too
grand, too gloomy, and what I style *most magnificently
uncomfortable*, the situation bad, the rooms, except one,
too small, and I want three or four more considerable
ones.

> Mrs Lybbe Powys, *Diaries*, 1776

Hagley Park, Worcestershire : I hope I shall not appear
either peevish, or self-opinion'd to say I was disappointed with Hagley. [It] is deficient of water and
gravel, two great charms. . . .

The house is ill situated, and ill-looking, and is
enter'd by a flight of steps, inconvenient and unsafe, in
summer, and winter. The inside is tawdrily and badly

fitted up with carving, gilding, Chinese paper, etc., and the hall is very inelegant. With light colour'd paint shou'd I instantly cover the Chinese paper; and in haste throw down the carved work of trumpets, cymbals, and wind mills.

3.7.1781

*

Easton Neston, Northamptonshire : I proposed a walk to Easton-Neston, the seat of Ld. Pomfret, built on the hill above the town; a great, staring, unpleasant dwelling, of neither comfort or content; surrounded by great offices, adorn'd by statues, and commanding an offensive view. Such a place I shou'd be tempted to . . . [*the sentence is unfinished*].

5th Viscount Torrington, *Diaries,* 2.7.1789

Lord Torrington was notoriously difficult to please.

§

Well, we have been to Longleat, and Longleat is indeed clean and comfortable and as fine as a great house can

be without that touch of good taste, the lack of which
one notices at every step. But there is a succession of
apartments, some of them approaching the palatial –
noble and spacious, with commodious corridors, and
bedrooms in the best economical style of the latest and
most up-to-date furnished lodgings. There are some
miserable cabinets, a deal of daubs enough to make
one spit, and only two pieces of china to envy.

> William Beckford, *Correspondence*, 12.9.1814 (from
> Boyd Alexander, *Life at Fonthill*, 1957)

*Narford Hall, Norfolk : Sir Andrew Fountaine amassed
a famous collection of porcelain and miscellaneous works
of art in the early eighteenth century. John, Lord Hervey
called it*

absolutely the prettiest trinket I ever saw. My Lord
Burlington could not make a better ragout of paintings,
statues, gilding and virtù!

> *Lord Hervey and His Friends*, ed. The Earl of Ilchester, 1952

and Lord Oxford :

It is a pretty box, a great deal of gilding and painting,
done by very bad hands [*Pellegrini no less*]. The library
is very smart and beauish, there are round the rooms
the heads of several learned men, but very ill done.

As for the china room, it was

a most wretched place, set out upon shelves like a shop,
no old china, a mere baby room.

> 2nd Earl of Oxford, *Account of a Journey*, 1732

George Vertue however thought differently. He called it :

a most rare cabinet of earthen ware, painted, guilded,
and adorned with great beauty and variety . . . and
arranged in the most elegant order that could be
imagined.

> George Vertue, *Note Books*, 1739 (*Walpole Society*, V, 1938)

Wycombe Abbey, Bucks: rebuilt for Lord Carrington by James Wyatt in 1798:

The Architect is exercising his *Shreds* of Gothic Genius in every possible quimp & Crank of wanton & extravagent foolery – the rooms are of different heights, some too low, others too Lofty, the Passages are immensely broad in proportion to the Rooms which are in general too narrow, the Chimney Pieces are very low & very small for size of the rooms. Mr W's object is an imitation of Ancient Times, which accord very indifferently with Modern Customs. Mr W hopes to finish it in four years from this time, when if POOR Lord Carrington survive – and Mr W has transferr'd Lord C's fortune into his own coffers, I should recommend it to be Call'd Rag Man's Castle.

Sarah Haslam, *Travel Journal,* 1802

Waddesdon Manor, Buckinghamshire : One day we drove over to lunch with Miss Alice Rothschild who had been a friend of Ethel Sands's mother. We were shown over the house, and all its priceless works of art. It seemed more oppressive even than an ordinary museum, which is after all open to the public. This, on the contrary, was guarded from human view. We were marshalled round the rooms by Miss Rothschild, and I was told by her 'not to touch' when my hand rested for a moment on a table.

I felt as if I was moving in the interior of a Louis XIV clock that would cease ticking if I stepped off the drugget that was laid across each room. A breath of criticism was indeed cried into my ear by Henry James; his basilisk gaze had absorbed the company of seven-foot-high footmen that waited on us, the hot-house flowers and the dish of enormous white strawberries that were in front of the plates. He looked up at the footmen, he looked down on the strawberries.

'Murder and rapine,' he said, 'would be preferable to this.'

So inhuman was the atmosphere of this private museum that none of us were directed to the place which is after all so necessary a provision even in a museum. When Howard Sturgess suggested asking one of the young giants where it was to be found, Henry James threw up his arms and said to him, 'Howard dear, what I thought was an Elysian dream you have made into a physiological fact.'

Lady Ottoline Morrell, *Early Memories*, April 1909

Evelyn Waugh summarized taste as the unostentatious, the simple, the perdurable, while lamenting that the English recognize the greatness of their heritage only when it is too late.

More even than the work of the great architects, I loved buildings that grew silently with the centuries, catching and keeping the best of each generation, while time curbed the artist's pride and the Philistine's vulgarity, and repaired the clumsiness of the dull workman. In such buildings England abounded, and, in the last decade of their grandeur, Englishmen seemed for the first time to become conscious of what before was taken for granted, and to salute their achievements at the moment of extinction.

Evelyn Waugh, *Brideshead Revisited*, 1945

Hospitality

The moral to be drawn from the quotations in this section seems to be that those entertainments where the host, or hostess, tries too hard to please, are less enjoyable than those which are al fresco, or upon a modest scale, whether the guests be royalty or mere commoners.

The Neville Feast : It was held in September 1465, at Cawood Castle, near York. It almost certainly lasted several days. Although its ostensible purpose was to celebrate the enthronement of George Neville as Archbishop of York, it must also have been planned as a demonstration of the power, wealth and solidarity of the great Neville clan. Seven bishops, ten abbots, twenty-eight peers, lawyers, clergy, aldermen and esquires travelled from all over the country to attend it. Since they all came with an appropriate number of attendants the total number of people involved (including those serving and waiting) was somewhere in the neighbourhood of 2,500 people; the food eaten included 113 oxen, 6 wild bulls, 1,000 sheep, 2,000 each of geese, pigs, and chicken, 12 porpoises and 4,000 cold venison pasties.

Mark Girouard, *Life in the English Country House*, 1978

'Twas never good days but when great tables were kept in large halls, the buttery-hatch always open; black jacks, and a good smell of meat and March beer; with dogs' turds and marrow bones as ornaments in the hall. These were signs of good housekeeping. I hate to see Italian fine buildings with no meat or drink in 'em.

Thomas Shadwell, *The Lancashire Witches*, 1681

Knole, Kent : In the old Duke's time [the groom of the chambers] said, the company us'd to be as innumerable as the apartments, and made us laugh by an instance of this, having desir'd the housekeeper to count the sheets she gave out, having delivered fourscore pairs, she said, she would count no longer.

December 1771

✳

Henley Park, Bucks : Perhaps you may have seen in the newspapers that our Fawley environs was then honour'd by the royal visitors .... [Mrs Freeman] most unluckily had been some time confined to her house with a violent cold; and the butler came running up to her dressing-room, saying, 'The King and Queen, Ma'am.' 'Don't alarm me, William' (you know her delicate manner); 'they are not coming here, but to Fawley Court, no doubt.' However another footman followed immediately, saying the carriages were just driving up, and he had got a good fire in the drawing-room. She had only time to say, 'A smart breakfast, William,' and to throw on a huge cloak, and was just down when the King, Queen, two Princesses, Lady Louisa Clayton, and two gentlemen entered. They stayed two hours and a half, talked incessantly, seemed vastly pleased, and knew every family and their concerns in the neighbourhood. Mrs Freeman said better than she did herself! The worst of these great visitors are that no servants must appear, and you are obliged to wait on them yourself; this, ill as she then felt, was very fatiguing; besides, not knowing the art, one must do it awkwardly. . . . But the King seeing Mrs Freeman was really ill, would not let her stir. . . . After breakfast the King said they must see the house. 'Certainly,' Mrs Freeman said, and was going to the door to attend them, but he kept her back, and shut her in, saying, 'You shall not go out with such a cold; we will go by ourselves.'

30.12.1785

*

Culham Court, Berkshire : Mr West had hot rolls brought from Gunter, wrapped in flannel, by relays of horsemen! The King said, 'Ah, Gunter, Gunter! I am glad you deal with Gunter, West: nobody like Gunter.' The King wiped his shoes carefully on entering, and on Mr West telling him not to mind, said, 'No, West, I am not going to carry dirt into any man's house.' . . . When they went over the apartments, the King, who always goes into every room, popped into one where the maid was dressing out the flowers, etc. She started up, and was greatly alarmed, but His Majesty laughed, and said to her, 'Don't be frightened; I won't steal any one thing.'

Mrs Lybbe Powys, *Diaries*, 26.11.1804

Berkeley Castle, Gloucestershire : The Prince of Wales on his late visit to Lord Berkeley at Berkeley Castle made those who received Him glad when it was over. Previous to His coming one of His pages arrived to prepare everything for Him. On being shown the room in which the Prince was to sleep He exclaimed, 'This the room, a gloomy room like this, it will not do.' The Chief Servant of Lord Berkeley observed, that Berkeley is an ancient not a modern building & the room they were in had been considered the best in it. The Page however demanded to see another and was shewn into an adjoining apartment, which had been intended for Him. 'This sd He, shall be the room for the Prince & I will sleep in the other,' which accordingly was settled.

One day the Prince having dined there at six o Clock Lady Berkeley did not ask Him to fix an Hour the following day but ordered the dinner to be ready at Six, & at that Hour the Prince was informed that dinner was ready. He sent word that He could not then dine, and the dinner was taken off the table, & they waited till eight o Clock before He made his appearance. He was there on a *Sunday* & Lady Berkeley asked Him whether He proposed to go to Church? To which he answered, 'That if she desired it, or it wd oblige Her He would go.' To this she made no reply & He did not go.

Vol. IV, 23.11.1807

*

The manner of living at *Dunmow*, a property of Sir George Beaumont, was as follows, viz:—

Fire laid in each Bedchamber at Seven o Clock in the morning.

Shaving water etc brought at 8 o Clock.

Breakfast at 9.

After breakfast Sir George & Alexander [artist guest] put on their painting aprons & went into the painting room where they passed their time till towards 3 o Clock.

They then walked out for an Hour or more & returned & dressed for dinner, which was always had at ½ past 4.

Tea was had at 7.

Then Sir George or Lady Beaumont read aloud, or occasionally they played at Whist to amuse old Lady Beaumont – Roasted apples were brought in – and abt ½ past ten or at Eleven o Clock they retired to bed.

J. Farington, *Diary*, Vol. V, 12.1.1808

At Batsford [Park, near Moreton-in-the-Marsh] Lord and Lady Redesdale with some young people were playing at Snap Dragon but having unfortunately put the Raisins into Spirits of Wine instead of Brandy, the Raisins bounced about and three ladies were set in a blaze, two were burnt most dreadfully and were obliged to keep their beds for many days.

Anne Rushout, Unpublished diaries, Christmas Day, 1813

Stoke Farm (Lord Sefton's), nr. Windsor, Berks : My life here is a most agreeable one. I am much the earliest riser in the House, and have above two hours to dispose of before breakfast, which is at eleven o'clock or even later. Then I live with myself again till about 3, when the ladies and I ride for 3 hours or so. . . . We dine at $\frac{1}{4}$ past seven, and the critics would say not badly. We drink in great moderation – walk out, all of us, before tea, and then crack jokes and *fiddle* till about $\frac{1}{2}$ past 12 or 1.

Thomas Creevey, *Papers*, 25.7.1823

A visit by foreigners to a nobleman's house in the middle of the last century could be daunting. The American Fay family dined at Oakley Park, Shropshire and were introduced to no one :

Two footmen in red plush breeches and bluecoats and silver buttons, and the groom of the chambers in black, received us in the vestibule, where we took off our cloaks. The dignitary in black preceded us through the hall and throwing open the door announced us as Mr and Mrs Fay, and the Misses Fay and Mr Fay. We found ourselves in a large and beautiful library, an elegant circle of ladies and gentlemen rose to meet us. Lady Harriet [Clive] received us with great dignity, and though no one was introduced every one spoke to us. It was not until the end of the evening that we knew who comprised the party. . . .

A. M. Fay, *Victorian Days in England*, 1852

The Edwardian Weekend :

Who among us today would really dress for church and dress for luncheon and dress for tea and dress again for dinner? Who among us would possess the endurance to relish all those meals, to relish all that tittle-tattle? Who today would care whether he was or was not invited to Upyatt Lacy or to West Warren? Who today prints or reads those lists of Saturday to Monday parties? The war has not been fought in vain. We have been released from false and exacting pretensions. We have our jumpers, our cocktails and our freedom. We can smoke pipes in Bond Street, and wear grey flannels in June. I do not regret that I was old enough to touch the fringe of Edwardian luxury. But I render thanks to Providence that I was also young enough to relish and share the wider liberties of our subsequent age. Let us be frank about it. The Edwardians were vulgar to a degree. They lacked style. They possessed only the hard glitter of their own electric light: a light which beat down pitilessly upon courtier, Ptarmigan, bridge scores, little enamel boxes, and plates and plates of food. They lacked simplicity, and their intricacies were expensive but futile. I, for one, prefer the wide circle of our simpler horizon, tumbled though it be by the waves of uncertainty. Nor, when all is said and done, can one forgive the Edwardians for their fundamental illusion. For it never dawned upon them that intelligence was of any value.

Harold Nicolson, *The Edwardian Weekend* (from *Small Talk*), 1937

A Weekend at Ditchingham, Norfolk:

I had a delightful room, big and comfortable – a regular old country-house room, with a dressing-room opening out of it. A nervous genial butler. Changed slowly and read *Pride and Prejudice*. The whole feeling of the place was like Miss Austen.

A good dinner – but Marsala only offered to drink. There were green claret-glasses and when I refused Marsala, the butler said to me, 'What will you drink?' I said, 'Claret – anything.' He said in a whisper, 'There's no claret opened.' So I drank barley-water. Afterwards very fine old port. . . .

After dinner Mr Carr took me off and we had a long genealogical talk. . . . He knew all about my relations and their exact fortunes. . . . Then we smoked in the Hall, and he gave me more information. Finally we could find no matches and he went and hunted in the dark – I could hear him tumble about – and conducted me to my bedroom. 'Here's your room – here's your dressing-room – all you want? Sleep well – you are welcome here, as one of the old stock!' I slept well, in a comfortable bed, the great cedar outside softly roaring in a strong S.W. wind.

A. C. Benson, *Diaries*, 11.9.1902

In January 1931 Mrs Ernest Simpson spent her first country-house weekend in Leicestershire:

We arrived at Melton Mowbray about five o'clock in the afternoon. A pea-soup fog had clamped down over the countryside, and as the car that met us at the station crawled into its cold, wet embrace, I found myself wishing that it would swallow me without a trace. At Thelma Furness's house we were met by her step-daughter, Averill, who told us that the rest of the party had been delayed on the road by the fog but were expected shortly. The house was a hunting-lodge of fairly recent date. It was spacious, and comfort was the keynote. It was furnished in typical country-house style – mahogany furniture and gay chintzes. We were taken into the drawing-room where there was a round table laid in front of the fireplace for tea. My cold was worse, if anything. I knew from the burning sensation of my skin that I had a slight temperature. More than anything else I wanted to slip upstairs to my room and go to bed. We made small conversation and had tea. A maid entered the drawing-room and quietly drew the curtains. Night had come. Still no sign or further word of the others. We sat and we sat and we sat. I saw Ernest glance nervously at his watch. Then about seven o'clock there was a sound of voices in the hall, and Thelma appeared with the two Princes. She introduced me to both of them. I summoned my fading courage and made my first curtsey to the Prince of Wales. To Ernest's surprise and my own it came off very well, as did my second one to Prince George. Thelma led us to the tea table, and we had tea all over again. Only then did I dare to scrutinise the two Princes.

The Duchess of Windsor, *The Heart has its Reasons*, 1956

Food and Drink

Wretched is the hall . . . each day in the week
There the Lord and Lady liketh not to sit.
Now have the rich a rule to eat by themselves
In a privy parlour . . . for poor men's sake,
Or in a chamber with a chimney, and leave the
    chief hall
That was made for meals, for men to eat in.

William Langland, *Piers Plowman*, 1360–99

As Mark Girouard has pointed out,

The widely-held and constantly repeated belief that family and household continued to eat together in the great hall until Elizabethan and even Jacobean days is based on nineteenth-century romanticism. From the second half of the fourteenth century onwards a great man increasingly ate in other rooms, and only returned to the great hall on special occasions, which became rarer and rarer.

Mark Girouard, *Life in the English Country House*, 1978

By King James I's reign the agricultural worker clearly had more common sense about diet than his descendant today who prefers sliced white bread to brown wholemeal.

The English husbandmen eat barley and rye brown bread, and prefer it to white bread as abiding longer in the stomach and not so soon digested with their labour, but citizens and gentlemen eat most pure white bread. . . . England, yea, perhaps one County thereof, hath more fallow deer than all Europe that I have seen. No kingdom in the world hath so many dove houses. Likewise brawn is a proper meat to the English, not known to others. English cooks, in comparison to other nations, are most commended for roasted meats.

Fynes Moryson, *An Itinerary*, 1617

But hark! the chiming clocks to dinner call;
A hundred footsteps scrape the marble hall:
The rich buffet well-coloured serpents grace,
And gaping Tritons spew to wash your face.
Is this a dinner? this a genial room?
No, 'tis a temple, and a hecatomb.
A solemn sacrifice, perform'd in state,
You drink by measure, and to minutes eat.

Alexander Pope, *Epistle to Lord Burlington*, 1733-4

Westmacott spoke of Lord Darnley as being very proud, with the high notions of the old nobility. At Cobham Hall, they dine at a *round* table, Lord Darnley sometimes sitting in one part & sometimes in another, & Lady Darnley always on His right Hand. When His Lordship is seated the Chaplain & Tutor, places Himself opposite to His Lordship & the *Children* next to the Chaplain. The manner of Lord Darnley is uniform, cold & reserved. He has £20,000 a year.

J. Farington, *Diary*, Vol. II, 10.3.1804

Altho' our King Jog [afterwards 1st Earl of Durham] *did* receive me so graciously yesterday . . . the sunshine was of very limited duration. You must know by a new ordinance *livery* servants are proscribed the dining-room; so our Michael and Frances [Taylor] were none the better for their two Cantley footmen, and this was the case too with Mrs General Grey, whom I handed out to dinner. . . . Soup was handed round – from where, God knows; but before Lambton stood a dish with one small haddock and three small whitings in it, which he instantly ordered off the table, to avoid the trouble of helping. Mrs Grey and myself were at least ten minutes without any prospect of getting any servant to attend to us, altho' I made repeated application to Lambton, who was all this time eating his own fish as comfortably as could be. So my blood beginning to boil, I said, 'Lambton, I wish you would tell me what quarter I am to apply to for some fish.' To which he replied in the most impertinent manner:— 'The servant, I suppose.' I turned to Mills and said pretty loud:— 'Now, if it was not for the fuss and jaw of the thing, I would leave the room and the house this instant'; and I dwelt on the damned outrage. Mills said, 'He hears every word you say'; to which I said, 'I hope he does'. . . . It was a regular scene. . . .

Thomas Creevey, *Papers*, Vol. II, 24.10.1825

England is the true land of contrasts – 'du haut et du bas' at every step. Thus, even in elegant houses in the country, coachmen and grooms wait at dinner, and are not always free from the odour of the stable.

Prince Pückler-Muskau, *English Tour*, 3.2.1827

The characters in Surtees's novels were not county magnates, but the lesser gentry living in north-country manor houses. Here Surtees is referring to the squirearchy of the old school:

... the larders, and the cellars, were expected to corre-
spond with the houses, the characters of the owners
depending a good deal on the strength of their taps,
while the conviviality of the dining-room always found
a hearty response in the servants' hall – masters and
butlers considering it a reproach to let anyone leave
the house sober. These hospitalities expired together,
French wines superseding the glorious old port, and
railways opening out other means of expenditure than
upon malt liquor for gratuitous distribution. A country
house in former days was little better than a great
unlicensed inn – everything was taken in that arrived,
and everybody had to be refreshed that came. We have
heard of a gentleman – not an M.P., or a man of large

fortune either – whose brewer's bill for a single year,
amounted to no less a sum than eight hundred pounds!

R. S. Surtees, *Plain or Ringlets*, 1860

The Edwardian Breakfast:

Only the really improper Edwardians had breakfast in
their rooms. The others met, on that Sunday morning,
in the dining-room. The smell of last night's port had
given place to the smell of this morning's spirits of
wine. Rows of little spirit lamps warmed rows of large
silver dishes. On a table to the right between the windows were grouped Hams, Tongues, Galantines, Cold
Grouse, ditto Pheasant, ditto Partridge, ditto Ptarmigan.
No Edwardian meal was complete without Ptarmigan.
Hot or cold. Just Ptarmigan. There would also be a
little delicate rectangle of pressed beef from the shop
of M. Benoist. On a further table, to the left between
the doors, stood fruits of different calibre, and jugs of
cold water, and jugs of lemonade. A fourth table contained porridge utensils. A fifth coffee, and pots of
Indian and China tea. The latter were differentiated
from each other by little ribbons of yellow (indicating
China) and of red (indicating, without *arrière pensée*,
our Indian Empire). The centre table, which was pre-
pared for twenty-three people, would be bright with
Malmaisons and toast-racks. No newspapers were, at
that stage, allowed.

Harold Nicolson, *The Edwardian Weekend* (from *Small Talk*),
1937

It was not until about 1849 or 1850 . . . that five o'clock
tea in the drawing-room was made an institution, and
then only in a few fashionable houses where the dinner
hour was as late as half-past seven or eight o'clock.

Georgiana Caroline Sitwell, *The Dew it lies on the Wood*
(from O. Sitwell, *Two Generations*, 1940)

Servants

In medieval times the household of a great prince or noble was immense. In the middle of the fourteenth century (according to Mark Girouard) Lord Berkeley may have had 300 servants at Berkeley Castle. One suspects that on the whole large households were happy establishments. Each servant had his own job. The lower servants had few responsibilities. Whereas class distinctions were paramount, class barriers were less in evidence than in the eighteenth and even nineteenth centuries.

The sons of the nobility were sent out to service in neighbouring households :

All the sons of the nobles acted as his servants, with downcast looks, nor dared they to look upward toward the heavens unless it so happened that they were addressing him [William Longchamp, Bishop of Ely]; if they attended to anything else they were pricked with a goad, which their lord held in his hand, fully mindful of his grandfather of pious memory, who, being of servile condition in the district of Beauvais, had, for his occupation, to guide the plough and whip up the oxen.

The Babees Book, 15th century

Some sixteenth-century lords were proud as Lucifer.

I will that he [the Clerk of the Kitchen] suffer none to stand unseemly with his back to my meat while it is at the range.

Lord Montague of Cowdray Castle,
Directions to his Household, c. 1590

By Queen Anne's reign, in ducal households:

The gentlemen servants no longer included elder, or even younger, sons of good county families. They were recruited from, at best, a respectable middle-class background – the sons of merchants, clergymen and army officers.

Mark Girouard, *Life in the English Country House*, 1978

Wesenham Hall, Norfolk: The old house-keeper has now been there one-and fifty years; the butler two- or three-and-thirty; poor Mrs. Jackson's maid, now Miss Jackson's, twenty-four, having been married to one of the footmen (their daughter is grown up, and is one of the housemaids) . . . 'tis really a pleasure to see them all so happy. I was surprised to see them all, except on Sundays, in green stuff gowns, and on my enquiring of Miss Jackson how they all happened to fix so on one particular colour, she told me a green camblet for a gown used for many years to be an annual present of her mother's to those servants who behaved well, and had been so many years in her family, and that now indeed, as they all behaved well, and had lived there much longer than the limited term, this was constantly their old master's New Year gift.

Mrs Lybbe Powys, *Diaries*, 1756

Battle Abbey, Sussex: We were permitted, till the family assemblage, to run into the house, catching a glympse of the lofty old hall, and one old chamber; and saw, yet a greater curiosity, the family butler, Mr Ingall, 103 years of age, who had been a post-boy in York, in Queen Anne's reign; and now, frequently, in a passion, gives warning, and threatens to quit his place: he was very deaf, else I wou'd have spoken to him; but we both bow'd to him; and his age bow'd him to us!

5th Viscount Torrington, *Diaries*, Vol. I, 20.8.1788

Hardwicke Court, Oxfordshire : A shocking accident. John Heath, our coachman, who had been at home some days ill of a fever, got up unknown to his family, came to our house, and threw himself down into our well in a fit of frenzy.

Mrs Lybbe Powys, *Diaries,* 25.6.1791

The late Mr Glover told me, he was dining once with Lord Townshend, when in the evening a bonfire was made near the house, on the account of some naval victory. They had in the room an American savage, who was in the greatest distress at the thought of being roasted, & eaten at the fire, which he concluded was made for him. They all tried to remove his fears; but in vain. They had no medium of language. At last Lord T took a piece of paper, & gave him a representation of a naval engagement. . . . In short he made him understand that the bonfire was a rejoicing for a naval victory.

William Gilpin to Mary Hartley, 13.11.1794

Directions to the Housemaid:

The sun comes into the Library very early. The window on that side of the bow must have the blind let down. The painted chairs must not be knocked against anything, or against one another. . . . To take turns of going to Church every other Sunday with the Laundry-maid.

Directions to the Butler:

Never to take any friend or stranger into the Pantry. Care of the key of the Plate.

Do. do. of bottle rack.

Susanna Whatman's *Housekeeping Book*, 1776–1800

This day I spoke to Mary abt. Her receiving the Sacrament on Christmas Day, which she told me she was much disposed to do. . . . She said she now lived in a State to receive the Sacrament with hope & comfort . . . that since she came to my House she and Sarah had not lived happily together, & while in a state of personal quarrel she did not think she could attend the Sacrament without impropriety. She said she had been most unhappy while this state of quarrelling continued, but that for their comfort they had for a long time lived as friends in a state of harmony. I said all that appeared to me proper strongly exhorting Her to reflect upon the evil consequences of living in such a state with anyone. She expressed Herself fully satisfied of the truth of what I sd.

J. Farington, *Diaries*, Vol. VII, 18.12.1814

Lambton Castle, Durham : says Lady Augusta Milbank to me yesterday, 'Do you know what happened last night?' 'Du tout', says I. 'Why,' says she, 'Mr Lambton rung the bell for water so long, that he went and rung the house bell, when his own man came; and upon saying something in his own justification which displeased the Monarch, he laid hold of a stick and struck him twice; upon which his man told him he could not stand that, and that if he did it again he should be obliged to knock him down. So the master held his hand and the man gave him notice he had done with him.'

Thomas Creevey, Papers, Vol. II, 23.9.1824

Corsham Court, Wilts : At one o'clock [the housekeeper] appeared again, and said she was afraid I should lose much time if I went to dinner at the inn, and that, if I would not be offended, she would propose to me to take part in her plain dinner. . . . [The invitation] was offered with so much delicacy. To complete our trio I found at table an old steward, who was as peevish and laconic as the good woman was friendly and talkative. To give you an idea of a Sunday dinner among this class of people I will tell you in what it consisted. First of all, there was a joint of lamb admirably roasted, on which I must observe that the lambs in England do not, as with us, consist of hardly anything but skin and bone, but have besides plenty of tender and sound flesh and fine fat; as for vegetables, we had the best potatoes and beans. After this came an apple pie with custard; to which a very delicate taste was imparted by the juice of some flower unknown to me. Gloucester cheese and very good ale concluded the whole.

Dr G. F. Waagen, Works of Art and Artists in England,
Vol. III, 1835

Petworth House, Sussex : A melancholy catastrophe at Petworth House. Five servants, very chilly, took a large brazier of charcoal into their sleeping room. They were all suffocated.

Elizabeth, Lady Holland to her Son, 6.2.1838

Knebworth Park, Hertfordshire : The domestic staff at Knebworth was a large one, as was usual in those days [the 1870s], and the etiquette observed was very rigid. The head servants took their meat in the Hall with the lower domestics and that part of the meal was eaten in complete silence, but with the advent of the pudding, the head servants took up their plates and solemnly marched with them into the Housekeeper's Room. Then, and then only, might the underlings speak. Our great amusement as children was to peep into the Hall during the solemnity of the meat course and try to make our special friends among the lower staff giggle. One of the housemaids, promoted to be my maid as I grew older . . . often told me of the hard time she had after her promotion as the senior domestics looked down upon this upstart risen from the ranks and made her life a misery.

Lady Emily Lutyens, *A Blessed Girl,* 1953

Belvoir Castle, Rutland : The cumbersome oil lamps of pre-electric light days [the 1880s] were a great source of trouble and expense, apart from the danger of fire which they sometimes caused owing to careless handling. In large houses men had to be specially told off to attend to the lamps. I remember the uncle of the present Duke of Rutland showing me the lamp-room at Belvoir full of gigantic barrels of oil; at the same time he told me that no less than six men were kept constantly employed at nothing else but looking after the lamps.

Lady Dorothy Nevill, *Leaves from the Note-Books of,* 1907

Madam,

I thank you for your enquiries about Irene Pethard's character while in my service as under-housemaid. Irene Pethard is sober, honest, God-fearing, and of a pleasant disposition. Her sole disqualification for promotion in my household is that she wears spectacles.

I am, Yours truly,

Madeleine Anderson (Lady).

Letter to the Editor's grandmother, dated 27 July 1911

Belvoir Castle, Rutland c. 1900 : The gong-man was an old retainer, one of those numberless ranks of domestic servants which have completely disappeared and today seem fabulous. He was admittedly very old. He wore a white beard to his waist. Three times a day he rang the gong – for luncheon, for dressing-time, for dinner.

He would walk down the interminable passages, his livery hanging a little loosely on his bent old bones, clutching his gong with one hand and with the other feebly brandishing the padded-knobbed stick with which he struck it. Every corridor had to be warned and the towers too, so I suppose he banged on and off for ten minutes, thrice daily.

Then there were the lamp-and-candlemen, at least three of them. . . . The water-men are difficult to believe in today. . . . They were the biggest people I had ever seen. . . . They had stubbly beards and a general Bill Sikes appearance. They wore brown clothes, no collars and thick baize aprons from chin to knee. On their shoulders they carried a wooden yoke from which hung two gigantic cans of water. They moved on a perpetual round. Above the ground floor there was not a drop of hot water, and not one bath. . . . Lastly, there were the watchmen who frightened many a newcomer to death. . . . All night they walked the passages, terraces and battlements. Yet no one really saw them. . . . Always if one woke in the night, as the fire flickered to its death, one would hear a padded foot on the gravel outside and a voice, not loud enough to waken but strong enough to reassure, saying, 'Past twelve o'clock. All's well!'

Lady Diana Cooper, *The Rainbow Comes and Goes*, 1958

Down in the steward's room the butler offered his arm gravely to the Duchess of Hull's maid, and conducted her to the place at his right hand. Lord Roehampton's valet did the same by Mrs Wickenden, the housekeeper. Mrs Wickenden of course, was not married, and her title was bestowed only by courtesy. The order of precedence was very rigidly observed, for the visiting maids and valets enjoyed the same hierarchy as their mistresses and masters; where ranks coincided, the date of creation had to be taken into account, and for this purpose a copy of Debrett was always kept in the housekeeper's room – last year's Debrett, appropriated by Mrs Wickenden as soon as the new issue had been placed in Her Grace's boudoir. The maids and valets enjoyed not only the same precedence as their employers, but also their names.

Vita Sackville-West, *The Edwardians*, 1930

Children

In the middle of the eighteenth century Frances Boscawen, a fond wife and mother, in a letter to her husband, Edward, Admiral of the Blue, serving overseas, recounts her daily routine with the children. She is writing from their home at Hatchlands, Surrey.

In all this I am accompanied by your two daughters, who are called every day at 6 by Nannie Humphreys. This (in respect to Fanny) is done by doctor's orders. He bid me send her out every morning in the early dew that she might outgrow the difference (not inconsiderable) that there is between her two collar bones. . . . We breakfast in your dressing-room. When 'tis over Miss Pitt (acting as governess) retires to her own devices and the girls remain to read and work. And while they work, I write. Here they are at this moment sitting by me, hemming pocket handkerchiefs for Mr Billy's [their brother's] coat pocket. They desire their duty to Papa. . . . After dinner all hands to feed the chickens, then to walk and then to settle in my dressing-room, where I am the worker and Miss Pitt the reader. This continues till near 8, when the girls go to bed, and we take our evening walk, which is generally out of the park.

Frances Boscawen, *Correspondence*, 9.6.1755

Moccas Court, Herefordshire, c. 1800 : When I was quite a child about 6 years old, my Mother (who hated governesses) had over from France a French Abbé, Monsieur Babey, an old man but turned out perfectly well. He never (wisely) interfered with our Protestant creed, taught French, geography, arithmetic, even the higher branches of it, was quite well conducted & used to ride an old pony every Sunday to Hereford to attend High Mass. He lived with us about 7 years I think, & went with my brother Charles to Leipzig, where he was sent to learn German before he went into the City House of business in Austin Friars.

Lady Duff Gordon to Mrs A. C. Master (unpubl.),
20.11.1872

Victorian children of the upper classes were disciplined more brutally than those of any other age. Augustus Hare's experience was not extraordinary. Shortly after his birth in 1834 his uncle Augustus Hare's widow wrote to his mother begging to be given the child. Mrs Hare's answer was very brief—

'My dear Maria, how very kind of you! Yes, certainly, the baby shall be sent as soon as it is weaned; and, if any one else would like one, would you kindly recollect that we have others.'

Another aunt, Esther Hare, undertook his early education.

Open war was declared at length between Aunt Esther
and myself. I had a favourite cat called Selma, which I
adored, and which followed me about wherever I went.
Aunt Esther saw this, and at once insisted that the cat
must be given up to her. I wept over it in agonies of
grief: but Aunt Esther insisted. My [adoptive] mother
was relentless in saying that I must be taught to give
up my own way and pleasure to others; and forced to
give it up if I would not do so willingly, and with many
tears, I took Selma in a basket to the Rectory [for Aunt
Esther was the wife of a clergyman]. For some days it
almost comforted me for going to the Rectory, because
then I possibly saw my idolised Selma. But soon there
came a day when Selma was missing: Aunt Esther had
ordered her to be . . . hung!

Augustus Hare, *The Years with Mother*, 1896

*Lord Curzon's treatment by his governess makes one's
hair stand on end:*

Kedleston Hall, Derbyshire c. 1870: In her savage
moments she was a brutal and vindictive tyrant; and I
have often thought since that she must have been
insane. She persecuted and beat us in the most cruel
way and established over us a system of terrorism so
complete that not one of us ever mustered up the
courage to walk upstairs and tell our father and mother.
She spanked us with the sole of her slipper on the bare
back, beat us with her brushes, tied us for long hours
to chairs in uncomfortable positions with our hands
holding a pole or a blackboard behind our backs, shut
us up in darkness, practised on us every kind of perse-
cution, wounding our pride by dressing us (me in
particular) in red shining calico petticoats (I was
obliged to make my own) with an immense conical

cap on our heads round which, as well as on our breasts
and backs, were sewn strips of paper bearing in enormous characters, written by ourselves, the words Liar,
Sneak, Coward, Lubber and the like. In this guise she
compelled us to go out in the pleasure ground and
show ourselves to the gardeners. . . .

She made me write a letter to the butler asking him
to make a birch for me with which I was to be punished
for lying and requesting him to read it out in the
Servants' Hall. . . . She forced us to confess to lies
which we had never told, to sins we had never com-
mitted, and then punished us savagely, as being self-
condemned. For weeks we were not allowed to speak
to each other or to a human soul.

Autobiographical Notes by Marquess Curzon of Kedleston,
quoted by Kenneth Rose in *Superior Person*, 1969

The enfant terrible *is an aggressive figure in fiction no less
than in fact.*

'I should have thought it was very nice to be called
a tart,' John argued, 'and anyway it's a word Ben often
uses about people.'

'Well, he's got no business to.'

'I like Ben more than anyone in the world. And I
should think he's cleverer too.'

'Now you know you don't like him more than your
mother.'

'Yes, I do. *Far* more.'

Tony felt that the time had come to cut out the cross
talk and deliver the homily he had been preparing.
'Now listen, John. It was very wrong of you to call
Nanny a silly old tart. First, because it was unkind to
her. Think of all the things she does for you every day.'

'She's paid to.'

'Be quiet. And secondly, because you were using a
word which people of your age and class do not use.

[74]

Poor people use certain expressions which gentlemen do not. You are a gentleman . . . .'

Evelyn Waugh, *A Handful of Dust*, 1934

Animals

Letters purporting to be written by one owner's dog to another's flew between Henrietta Howard's Marble Hill and Horace Walpole's Strawberry Hill. Horace was infatuated with his dogs, as this letter to his crony Horace Mann testifies:

My dear Sir, how I am obliged to you for your poem! Patapan is so vain with it, that he will read nothing else; I only offered him a Martial to compare it with the original, and the little coxcombe threw it into the fire, and told me, 'He never heard of a lapdog's reading Latin; that it was very well for house-dogs and pointers that live in the country, and have several hours upon their hands: for my part,' said he:

> 'I am so nice, who ever saw
> A Latin book on my sofa?
> You'll find as soon a Bible there
> Or recipe for pastry ware.'

Horace Walpole to Sir Horace Mann, *Correspondence*,
12.10.1743

The architect Earl of Pembroke left directions in his will that:

those horses that are at grass may be allowed hay where there is not grass sufficient and such horses as by age or other accidents may be rendered unable to feed themselves I would have such horses only to be shot without being carried out of the walls of Wilton Park or Courts there till dead and I do direct that some trusty servant may be employed to see the same executed.

Will of Henry Herbert, 9th Earl of Pembroke, 1750

Cumberland Lodge, Windsor Park : The Duke has wild beasts here, and I saw an ostrich walking in the lawn near the house.

Dr Richard Pococke, *Travels*, 15.8.1754

Gosfield Hall, Essex : the seat of Lord Clare, who has an exceeding fine park: but I take the opportunity of mentioning him here, chiefly on account of a stroke in agriculture, most unusual in Essex; which is the using oxen instead of horses, for all the purposes of draught.

Arthur Young, *A Southern Tour*, 1767

I must celebrate the sense of Fidèle, Mrs Damer's terrier. Without making the slightest gesture, her mistress only said to her, 'Now, Fidèle, you may here jump on any chair you please.' She instantly jumped on the settee; and so she did in every room for the whole two days she stayed. This is another demonstration to me that dogs understand even language, so far as it relates to their own affairs.

Horace Walpole to Miss Mary Berry, 6.8.1789

Blenheim Palace, Oxon : What shock'd me much, was
to hear the firing of guns, and to see a set of Jacobins
arm'd against the national guards – the birds – Oh
fye! – What, for a few cherries, destroy all the song-
sters? And here will they come to perish. 'Stretch
forth, Marlborough, thy hand of mercy, and of pity;
and let not infamous slaughter prevail.'

5th Viscount Torrington, Diaries, Vol. III, 5.7.1792

Newstead Abbey, Nottinghamshire :

Near this spot
Are deposited the Remains of one
Who possessed Beauty without Vanity,
Strength without Insolence,
Courage without Ferocity,
And all the Virtues of Man without his Vices.
This Praise, which would be unmeaning Flattery
If inscribed over human ashes,
Is but a just tribute to the Memory of
BOATSWAIN, a Dog,
Who was born at Newfoundland, May, 1803,
And died at Newstead Abbey, Nov. 18, 1808.

Lord Byron, 'Epitaph to Boatswain on his monument
placed on the site of the High Altar of the ruined Abbey'

Squires, Good and Bad

*The former assuredly outnumber the latter but are usually
the less entertaining.*

Seaton Delaval, Northumb. : Catastrophes dogged the
Delavals and their home. Long before the house was
finished Admiral George Delaval was thrown from his
horse one evening after dinner and killed outright.
His nephew Francis Blake took over. During his life-

time events proceeded smoothly enough until he fell in a drunken fit under the portico. He was succeeded in 1752 by Sir Francis, 'the gayest and most accomplished Lothario of his age'. In his reign were staged the maddest, most hilarious entertainments conceivable – tournaments, rope dances and masquerades. Drunkenness, debauchery, extravagance and fun were the order of day after day. Delavals died of falls, drink, sex and, as has been recorded, kicks.

J. L-M, *English Country Houses, Baroque,* 1970

Houghton Hall, Norfolk : Only imagine that I here every day see men, who are mountains of roast beef, and only seem just roughly hewn out into the outlines of human form, like the giant-rock at Pratolino! I shudder when I see them brandish their knives in act to carve, and look on them as savages that devour one another. . . . Why, I'll swear I see no difference between a country gentleman and a sirloin; whenever the first laughs, or the latter is cut, there run out just the same streams of gravy!

Horace Walpole to John Chute, *Correspondence,* 20.8.1743

Jack Mytton :

He was exceedingly kind to his servants, and readily pardoned derelictions of duty when he found that the offender's repentance was sincere. But the grounds on which he chose his people were often peculiar. 'In once hiring a keeper, he did not go so much upon character and experience as the applicant's ability to thrash a certain sweep, that was in the habit of trespassing in the Halston covers. A trial was accordingly agreed to, and the new man put upon his watch. In due course, the sweep made his appearance, and after a long fight was well licked. The keeper's engagement was ratified at once, as the sweep was thoroughly satisfied – and the sweep was Mytton himself.'

> J. Timbs and A. Gunn, *Abbeys. Castles and Ancient Halls*, quoting Nimrod, 1872

Halston Hall, Shropshire : When [Jack Mytton] was a mere boy he lived at the rate of £800 a year – exactly double his allowance. Finding that the sum which was awarded him was quite inadequate, young Mytton wrote to Lord Eldon, as Lord Chancellor, requesting an increase of income, as he was going to be married! The boy was then only fourteen years of age! The reply of his legal guardian was sufficiently laconic:— 'Sir, if you cannot live on your allowance, you may starve; and, if you marry, I will commit you to prison.'

C. J. Apperley, *Memoirs of the Life of John Mytton*, 1837

[He] was a man of great physical strength and foolhardy courage, with an inordinate love of conviviality and a strongly developed taste for practical joking. He was a daring horseman and a splendid shot. . . . On [one] occasion he drove a tandem at night across country for a wager, and successfully surmounted a sunk fence three yards wide, a broad deep drain, and two stiff quickset hedges. He would sometimes strip to the shirt to follow wild fowl in hard weather; and once is said to have followed some ducks *in partibus naturalibus*. One night he even set fire to his night-shirt in order to

frighten away the hiccoughs. His average allowance was
from four to six bottles of port daily, which he com-
menced in the morning while shaving. Owing to his
reckless way of living Mytton lost his entire fortune,
and his effects at Halston were sold up. . . . He died of
delirium tremens in the King's Bench Prison aged 37.

Dictionary of National Biography, John Mytton 1796–1834

Relations between squire and parson have always been
equivocal, often distinguished by hauteur on one side and
subservience on the other.

I . . . wish that the clergy could live together in their
own communities, for I allways objected to their
society over the board:— as should they prove proud,
and formal, it was disgusting; and if frisky, it was even
more disgusting.

5th Viscount Torrington, *Diaries*, 1791

While Mr Carr [of Ditchingham Hall, Norfolk] and I
were sitting in the hall, not far from the front door,
which had glass panes, there came a seedy frowsy
parson and rang. Mr C looked up: 'Oh, here's our
Vicar, Scudamore, a very good fellow, but an awful
bore – he is always coming and hanging about here.
Don't take any notice of him. Look at this.' No one
answered the bell, and Mr Scudamore stood looking
in meekly upon us. At last after ten minutes we saw
him fumbling at the bell again. Mr Carr went and
opened it, and shook hands and introduced me.
Mr Scudamore a shy-looking owlish man, overgrown
with hair, badly dressed in dirty oily clothes – un-
brushed and unkempt. Mr Carr said – sharply but
good-humouredly and very courteously: 'Now, sir,
what do you want of me?'

A. C. Benson, *Diaries*, 13.9.1902

Petworth House, Sussex: The 6th Duke of Somerset (1662–1748):

He mulcted his daughter Charlotte £20,000 of her inheritance for having sat down in his presence. His domestics observed him by signs, and, when he travelled, the country roads were scoured by outriders, whose duty it was to protect him from the gaze of the vulgar.

Dictionary of National Biography

At meals they served him on bended knee.

The 9th Earl of Pembroke:

'Often mad and always very odd' was the verdict on Lord Herbert of Duchess Sarah [Marlborough]. . . . Eccentric he undoubtedly was. One form of eccentricity all but deprived him of his life. He became a fanatical vegetarian to the extent of practically starving himself to death. Parisian society was much astounded to see him walking the streets of their city – this was in 1729 – wearing a bag wig, which he treated as a knapsack and kept filled, not with hair, but watercress and beetroot, which he would extract and nibble at regular intervals.

J. L-M, Earls of Creation, 1962

Claydon House, Bucks: Ralph, 2nd Earl Verney (d. 1791), was as attractive as he was improvident. His generosity to and popularity with his tenants and neighbours was remarkable. He was incapable of withholding help and money whenever they were demanded of him. . . . Music and the arts were his obsession. His coach-and-six was escorted round the country by 'a brace of tall negroes, with silver French horns . . . perpetually making a noise, like Sir Henry Sidney's Trompeters in the days of Elizabeth, bloweing very joyfully to behold and see,' according to a description by a friend of Lord Verney. . . . His architectural

schemes utterly exhausted his own considerable fortune. . . . Towards the end of his life . . . he went bank-
rupt, and nearly everything in the house was sold. He
was obliged to escape to France to avoid his creditors.

There is a pathetic legend that once, during the long
period when the huge, unfinished house was empty
and shut up, a stable boy happened to peer through a
cobwebbed window. To his surprise he recognized the
Earl, then an old man, wandering disconsolately among
the desolate scenes of his former grandeur. His master
had, he explained when questioned, come down in a
hamper from London, and then hidden himself in the
house. The boy borrowed a bed and mattress from the
rectory, gave him something to eat, and kept him for
weeks concealed in the house.

National Trust Guide Book to *Claydon House*, 1974

Shipton Court

Medmenham Abbey, Bucks : This Abbey is now become
remarkable by being hired by a set of gentlemen [Sir
Francis Dashwood, Lord Sandwich, Sir W. Stanhope,
Bubb Dodington, George Selwyn and others], who
have erected themselves into a sort of fraternity of
Monks, & pass two days in every month there. Each
has his cell, in which indeed is little more than a bed.
They meet to drink, tho the rule is pleasure, & each

is to do whatever he pleases in his own cell, into which they may carry Women. . . . Over the door is written this Sentence from Rabelais, 'Fais ce que voudras'.

Horace Walpole, *Visits to Country Seats*, 1763

Later Walpole was to write :

politics had no sooner infused themselves among these rosy anchorites than dissensions were kindled, a false brother arose, who divulged the arcana and exposed the good Prior [Dashwood] in order to ridicule him as Minister of the Finances.

The 'false brother' was John Wilkes, who let loose a baboon while Lord Sandwich was conducting a ceremony of invoking the devil, an act of treachery which so unnerved the celebrant that it was never forgiven.

Westall I called on in even'g & drank tea – He told me that when He was at Lord Oxford's at Eywood in Herefordshire the last Autumn Lady Holland was spoken of. She had been there upon a visit & was very little liked. At dinner she had a foreigner a Servant standing behind Her Chair who tasted what came from each dish that she called for, & set it before Her or not as He conceived she wd or not approve its quality – Her bed was made by two of Her *Men Servants* as she sd our women do not know how to make a bed. – She appears to be altogether a sensualist.

Vol. III, 4.9.1806

*

Two Gentlemen from the neighbourhood came to dinner [at Coleorton, Leics]. . . . These gentlemen mentioned several particulars of the singularities of the present Sir Henry Harpur Crewe of Calke in Derbyshire. He is shy of communication to such an excess that He sometimes delivers his orders to His servants *by letter*. At dinner He sits down alone at a table

[83]

covered for several persons, and after dinner glasses
are placed as if for company and He takes His wine in
that form, but does not allow any servant to wait in
the room. . . . He keeps a pack or packs of Hounds, but
does not himself hunt, yet with all His unwillingness
to communicate He has pleasure in listening to His
Huntsmen while He gives an account of each Chase.

J. Farington, *Diary*, Vol. VII, 30.10.1812

*Hatfield House, Herts : Lord Cranborne lost the election
for the St Albans division.*

Lord Cranborne stood in the doorway first as if he
could not summon up enough courage to come in, but
Lady Salisbury called out to him, and he just came and
passed through, shaking his father's hand on the way.
They all tried to seem in high spirits. . . . After dinner
we all proceeded to the drawing-room to hear their
news, Gwenny in a very excited voice telling it all to
Lord Salisbury, who sat with tears in his eyes the whole
evening. They say it was the Catholic vote that lost
them the seat, as there are 1600 Roman Catholics in
Darwen and they all voted against him. . . .

I think it made it much better at Hatfield having
them all there, and Lady Salisbury said she did not
care in the least, but stood in the middle of the room
exclaiming in a loud voice, 'Damn the Catholics! Damn
the Catholics!' Frances and Eustace say she took a drop
too much to keep her up and that towards the end of
the evening she could hardly walk straight.

Lady Emily Lutyens, *A Blessed Girl*, 15.7.1892

Worship

Attendance by the squire at the parish church or family prayers was not unaccompanied by a due sense of his proper station in the social hierarchy.

To church, and had a good plain sermon. At our coming in the country-people all rose with so much reverence; and when the parson begins, he begins, 'Right worshipfull and dearly beloved' to us.

Samuel Pepys, *Diary*, 4.8.1661

Nobody presumes to stir till Sir Roger is gone out of the church.

Joseph Addison, *Sir Roger de Coverley* in the *Spectator*, 1711–12

And now the chapel's silver bell you hear,
That summons you to all the pride of prayer:
Light quirks of music, broken and uneven,
Make the soul dance upon a jig to Heaven . . .
On painted ceilings you devoutly stare,
Where sprawl the saints of Verrio or Laguerre,
On gilded clouds in fair expansion lie,
And bring all paradise before your eye.
To rest, the cushion and soft dean invite,
Who never mentions hell to ears polite.

Alexander Pope, *Epistle to Lord Burlington*, 1733–4

Plas Newydd, Anglesey : I shou'd mention that in Ld Uxbridge's chapel are kept wheels, carriages, and all kind of lumber; and that it stinks, most abundantly, of drying sea-fish:

How devout an age do we live in!!

5th Viscount Torrington, *Diaries*, Vol. I, 12.7.1784

The atmosphere of the Edwardian dining-room at nine-thirty was essentially daring. A pleasant sense of confederacy and sin hung above the smell of the spirit-lamps. For had they not all been brought up to attend family prayers? And had they not all eluded that obligation? It was true, of course, that the host and hostess, with their niece, had at nine proceeded to the family chapel and heard the butler reading a short collect for the day. But the guests had for their part evaded these Victorian obligations.

Harold Nicolson, *The Edwardian Weekend* (from *Small Talk*), 1937

The Vyne, Hampshire : Before breakfast, at 8.45 precisely, a sort of school bell rang, and we all trooped into the chapel for prayers, that is to say, the Chutes, I, the headmaster and mistresses of the school billeted here – the boys are now on holiday – the matron, followed by five servant girls in uniform. Mr Chute read the prayers, and the schoolmaster alone read the responses in so loud and aggressive a voice that I guessed he hated him. A sort of sparring match ensued. However it was all over in ten minutes. I liked it, but it is the first time I have ever attended Protestant prayers in a country house.

J. L-M, *Prophesying Peace*, 17.12.1944

Daily Bread

There is little doubt that boredom gnawed at the vitals of courtiers and socialites when they were in the country for any length of time. Not all of them were driven to such desperate expedients as Sidney's sister, Pembroke's mother.

She was very salacious, and she had a Contrivance that in the Spring of the yeare, when the Stallions were to leape the Mares, they were to be brought before such a part of the house [Wilton], where she had a *vidette* (a

hole to peepe out at), to look on them and please herselfe with their Sport; and then she would act the like
sport herselfe with *her* stallions. One of her great
Gallants was Crooke-back't Cecill, Earl of Salisbury.

John Aubrey, *Brief Lives*, 17th century

I have not yet been a day in the country, and I am as
weary of it as if I had been a prisoner there seven year.

William, 3rd Earl of Pembroke, 1601

Euston Hall, Suffolk : During my stay here with Lord
Arlington, near a fortnight, His Majesty came almost
every second day with the Duke, who commonly
returned to Newmarket, but the King often lay here,
during which time I had twice the honour to sit at
dinner with him, with all freedom. It was universally
reported that the fair Lady – – – – was bedded one of
these nights, and the stocking flung, after the manner
of a married bride; I acknowledge she was for the most
part in her undress all day, and that there was fondness
and toying with that young wanton; nay, it was said,
I was at the former ceremony; but it is utterly false; I
neither saw nor heard of any such thing whilst I was
there, though I had been in her chamber, and all over
that apartment late enough, and was myself observing
all passages with much curiosity. However it was with
confidence believed she was first made *a Miss*, as they
call these unhappy creatures, with solemnity at this
time.

John Evelyn, *Diary*, 9 and 10.10.1671

Health fuss was a favourite relaxation :

Last night I was terribly tormented with my itching,
and I am now sore again, which I should not have been,
if I had gone on with using the deers' suet; but I am
resolved to bear it, being satisfied that any greasy thing
repels; and when the smarting was ceased, I was not

so well in my stomach. But I am sure whatever I do, I can never be well. And at my age, as Sir William Temple says, the play is not worth the candles.

Sarah, Duchess of Marlborough to her granddaughter,
Diana, Duchess of Bedford, 24.9.1734

A busy day at Hatchlands, Surrey:

Affairs of the farm, of the garden, of the house. Directing Woodroffe to cheat Jo Gill of all the rotten dung – the said Jo to be content with the long dung. Then a chapter of apples and pears. Then (to Waite) a chapter of honeysuckle and laurels. Then to old Betty to make war upon the thistles in the Park, if any yet remain. Then to Mrs Whaley, for within-doors, shifts, rubbers, and kitchen table-cloths to cut out, lest my damsels degenerate into idleness, which is the root of all evil. Then *one* has a little bill, and t'other would be glad of a year's wages; then old Bronze wants some money, and Master Taylor must have the land tax. Then I must muster the brick carts; and I have also with my own hands composed a table for their regulation in my absence.

Fanny Boscawen to Admiral Boscawen, 14.10.1756

Does Mary cough in the night? two or three snails boiled in her barley water . . . might be of great service to her.

Mrs Delany to a friend, 1758

Chatsworth, Derbyshire : The Duke of Devonshire keeps two public days in a week; it is the etiquette of the family to return no visits in the County.

Horace Walpole, *Visits to Country Seats*, 1760

It is still the etiquette of the family to return no visits in the County.

Court-of-Hill, Shropshire : The roads about here are wonderful to strangers. Where they are *mending*, as they *call it*, you travel over a bed of loose stones, none of less size than an octavo volume; and where not mended, 'tis like a staircase. There are turnpikes – some of the roads not better than where we have none, but some are good. . . . They appear unfit for ladies travelling, but they mind them not. . . . So I mounted 'Grey', Mr Powys's great horse – luckily a native of Shropshire – and up I went the tremendous hill before mentioned. The fashion here is to ride double. How terribly vulgar I've thought this; but what will not fashion render genteel. 'Tis here thought perfectly so. As to carriages, they make nothing of going a dozen miles to dinner, tho' own to being bruised to death, and quite *deshabbiller'd* by jolts they must receive.

Mrs Lybbe Powys, Diaries, 1771

Lord Polwarth had a rib removed, without an anaesthetic of course, in 1780 :

Hunter [the surgeon] says he will cut me no more, for on two trials he can neither make me shrink nor change colour. Gough [his lordship's valet] most valiantly shut both eyes; and if he had not held fast by my arm he would have dropped; he pretended to hold the water glass, but soon began to totter, so helped myself; his phyz would have made a good picture: I neither bawled nor uttered, but I whispered, 'Oh dear!'

Joyce Godber, *The Marchioness Grey of Wrest Park*, 1968

Mr Cole says you must cut a bit of the coarsest brown paper, which you know is made of tar (or pitch) hemp, etc., the shape of your ears, and cover each ear with it at night, wearing it under your nightcap, and persist in this a long time. He vows it will cure your deafness.

Fanny Boscawen, *Correspondence*, 23.9.1790

Here we are [in a small house at Bookham], undisturbed, and undisturbing. . . . He [M. d'Arblay] works in his garden, or studies English or mathematicks, while I write. When I work at my needle, he reads to me; and we enjoy the beautiful country around us in long and romantic strolls, during which he carries under his arm a portable garden-chair, lent us by Mrs Locke, that I may rest as I proceed. He is extremely fond, too, of writing, and makes from time to time, memorandums of such memoirs, poems, and anecdotes as he recollects, and I wish to have preserved.

Fanny Burney, *Diary and Letters*, March 1794

Deene Park, Northants : One evening I gave a dinner-party to which I had invited some very dull neighbours, Mr and Mrs H . . . . Aubrey Coventry was staying at Deene, and he suggested playing a joke on Mr H, a very pompous, snobbish person, who 'dearly loved a lord'. Aubrey accordingly dressed himself up as a woman. He was laced into the cook's stays, and my sister-in-law lent him one of her exquisite tea-gowns.

He wore an effective wig, and I must say he made a very striking-looking woman. He was introduced to the Hs as Lady Aubrey Coventry, and sat between Mr H and John Vivian at dinner. Mr H talked a great deal to 'Lady Aubrey', who told me afterwards that out of sheer mischief he kept treading on Mr H's foot all through dinner, and he wickedly enjoyed watching the growing embarrassment of that gentleman's face!

When the ladies retired, Mrs H pounced on 'Lady Aubrey', and began to get so confidential that poor Aubrey was quite confused, and pleading sudden indisposition he went to his room. A few hours afterwards, clothed in his own garments, he was dancing at the ball which took place later in the evening, and I believe the Hs remained in happy ignorance of 'Lady Aubrey's' real identity.

Countess of Cardigan, *Recollections*, 1909

Games, Sports, and Pursuits

Sport was the universal be-all and end-all of country-house life down to 1939. In a few scattered pockets of the country it still is so today. It is only fair to say that the art and expertise of venery was stronger than the desire to kill.

Other [recreations] inflame the hot spirits of young men with roving ambition, love of war and seeds of anger; but the exercise of hunting neither remits the mind to sloth nor . . . hardens it to inhumanity; but rather inclines men to good acquaintance and generous society.

The Gentleman's Recreation of 1697

*Trophies of the chase were the time-honoured adornment
of the lesser gentry's walls:*

The Walls of his great Hall are covered with the Horns
of several kinds of Deer that he has killed in the Chace,
which he thinks the most valuable Furniture of his
House, as they afford him frequent Topicks of Dis-
course, and show that he has not been idle. At the
lower End of the Hall, is a large Otter's Skin stuffed
with Hay, which his Mother ordered to be hung up
in that manner, and the Knight looks upon it with
great Satisfaction, because it seems he was but nine
Years old when his Dog killed him. A little Room
adjoining to the Hall is a kind of Arsenal filled with
Guns of several Sizes and Inventions, with which the
Knight has made great Havock in the Woods, and
destroyed many thousands of Pheasants, Partridges
and Woodcocks. His Stable Doors are patched with
Noses that belonged to Foxes of the Knights own
hunting down. Sir Roger showed me one of them that
for Distinction Sake has a Brass Nail struck through it,
which cost him about fifteen Hours riding, carried
him through half a dozen Counties, killed him a Brace
of Geldings, and lost above half his Dogs. This the
Knight looks upon as one of the greatest Exploits of
his Life.

J. Addison, *Sir Roger de Coverley* in the *Spectator*,
1711-12

The Glorious Revolution Jubilee at Holkham, Norfolk:

Got to Holkham about 9 in the evening. Mr Coke
received the company at the door of the Saloon. The
grand suite illuminated in a capital style. . . . Dancing
in the Saloon and Statue Gallery, cards in three of the
other rooms. The Library & the rest for conversation,
etc. Refreshments at intervals. A cold supper with hot
soups and game at 2 o'clock. Excellent wines of all

sorts. A horse-shoe table in the north dining-room where Mrs C supped. Many other tables below in the Billiard Room & audit room – in the style of the Pantheon Masque suppers. The ladies ought to have supped first for by the whole company attempting to sit together there was some confusion. . . . In going up the steps of the Egyptian Hall a transparent painting of the P. Feathers presented itself with this motto: Liberty is our Cause.

Sylas Neville, Diary, 5.11.1788, ed. B. Cozens-Hardy,
1950

Packington Hall, Warwickshire : P. Park is a dead flat; and the new church building on the spot, is a wretched erection; the whole park is dotted by low stone pillars, which are the roving butts that Lord A[ylesford] shoots his arrows at; a sport of which he is furiously fond, and a most capital performance – perhaps the best gentleman archer in the kingdom.

5th Viscount Torrington, Diaries, Vol. II, 28.6.1789

Holkham, Norfolk : Though not much of a sportsman yourself, you may be living with those who are, and I suppose it would be incorrect to write a letter from hence – the day after the first battue – without mentioning that 780 head of game were killed by ten guns, and that 25 woodcocks formed a grand feature in the chase.

Viscountess Anson to Thomas Creevey, 5.11.1822,
(Creevey Papers)

The two most famous shots in England, are Captain de Roos and Mr Osbaldistone. They shot for a wager of a thousand pounds, which is not yet decided. Neither missed once; and Captain de Roos's birds never fell twelve paces from the spot, and scarcely fluttered, but dropped like stones almost the moment he fired. Never did I see such admirable shooting. A pretty little spaniel belonging to the [Pigeon] Club fetched every pigeon,

and performed his duty like a machine, without either
delay, neglect, or hurry. At last the whole party shot for
a golden vase of two hundred pounds value (the annual
prize of the Club), which was won by Captain de Roos.

16.6.1828

*

Here, however, people are so little shamed of the most
'crasse' self-love, that an Englishman of rank once
instructed me that a good fox-hunter must let nothing
stop him, or distract his attention when following the
fox; and if his own father should be thrown in leaping
a ditch, and lie there, should, he said, 'if he couldn't
help it,' leap his horse over him, and trouble himself
no more about him till the end of the chase.

Prince Pückler-Muskau, *English Tour*, 8.7.1828

Deene Park, Northants: My hunting recollections
would not be complete without including among them
the occasion in '73 when I went to a meet at Belvoir,
and met His Majesty King Edward VII, then Prince
of Wales, who was staying at the Castle. I was riding
my famous horse 'Dandy', who won the Billesdon
Coplow Stakes at Croxton Park, and that morning I
was much exercised in my mind about a proposal of
marriage I had just received from Disraeli. My uncle
Admiral Rous, had said to me, 'My dear, you can't
marry that damned old Jew,' but I had known Disraeli all my life, and I liked him very well. He had,
however, one drawback as far as I was concerned, and
that was his breath – the ill odour of politics perhaps!
In ancient Rome a wife could divorce her husband if
his breath were unpleasant, and had Dizzy lived in
those days his wife would have been able to divorce
him without any difficulty. I was wondering whether
I could possibly put up with this unfortunate attribute
in a great man, when I met the King, who was graciously pleased to ride with me. In the course of our

conversation I told him about Disraeli's proposal and asked him if he would advise me to accept it, but the King said he did not think the marriage would be a very happy one.

Countess of Cardigan, *Recollections*, 1909

Crabbet Park, Sussex: [Lady Anne Blunt] was a passionate lover of horses and it was reported that she went to bed fully equipped for riding – top boots and all – in order that she might be ready to ride in the early hours of the morning. . . . In spite of their [the Blunts'] numberless horses I should say they got as little pleasure from them as possible. As is the case with most luxuries, they are made slaves to their horses instead of the other way round. Though they ride every day, from the fuss that is made about the horses you would suppose that it was a very unusual thing to go for a ride.

June 1892

*

Terling Place, Sussex: After dinner we all played the most exciting game that ever was invented, called

Tiddleywinks. It consists in flipping counters into a bowl, and being a good number we played at two tables, one table against another, and the excitement was tremendous. I assure you everyone's character changes at Tiddleywinks in the most marvellous way. To begin with, everyone begins to scream at the top of their voices and to accuse everyone else of cheating. Even I forgot my shyness and howled with excitement.

Lady Emily Lutyens, *A Blessed Girl*, 24.4.1892

Blankney, Lincolnshire: We attended stables, as we attended church, in our best clothes, thereby no doubt showing the degree of respect due to horses, no less than to the deity: but afterwards, before luncheon, we changed into ordinary clothes. Though children object strongly to changing and especially to washing their hands yet on these occasions, how hard, and with what delight, I used to scrub them, seeking to rid them of the horses' slaver.

Sir Osbert Sitwell, *The Scarlet Tree*, 1946

Open to the Public

In the seventeenth and eighteenth centuries a gentleman could usually obtain admittance to a country house, no matter how grand, provided his tenue was correct and his travelling carriage impressive enough. The reception he got from owners and servants, agreeable and disagreeable, varied.

Audley End, Essex: Up by four o'clock: Mr Blayton and I took horse and straight to Saffron Walden, where at the White Hart, we set up our horses, and took the master of the house to shew us Audley End House, who took us on foot through the park, and so to the house,

where the house-keeper shewed us all the house, in
which the stateliness of the ceilings, chimney-pieces,
and form of the whole was exceedingly worth seeing.
He took us into the cellar, where we drank most admirable drink, a health to the King. Here I played on
my flageolette, there being an excellent echo.

Samuel Pepys, *Diary*, 27.2.1660

Dyrham Park, Gloucestershire : Mr Powell and I prepare matters for our journey today to Mr Blathwayt's
with the ladies. Hired a chaise and a pair of horses for
which we have 10s and 4s for the chaise. Upon the road
I was very uneasy to see Mr Powell so much taken
notice of more than myself. Mr Blathwayt's house is a
very handsome one . . . We saw all the waterworks
play which were very agreeable and delightful. At one
side of the gardens there is a wilderness of high large
trees in which there are a great many agreeable shades.

In one of them we made our dinner of some cold
things we brought and sat down upon the grass for two
or three hours. In this time Mrs Marshall showed a
great disregard of me and love for Mr Powell; particularly she refused me a kiss when she gave him one
immediately after. This put me into such a confusion
and uneasiness that I could not bear it and was forced
to take a walk by myself among the trees. Nor could I
prevent the tears gushing out, that I was forced to be
absent almost an hour.

Dudley Ryder, *Diary*, 1.6.1716

One circumstance I shall not omit, which is, the excessive insolence of the porters at the park-gate [at
Blenheim], and at that into the courtyard; for I was a
witness to their abusing a single gentleman in a very
scurrilous manner, for not feeing them after giving the
house-porter half a crown for seeing it.

Arthur Young, *A Southern Tour*, 1767

Holkham Hall, Norfolk: We had a breakfast at Holkham in the genteelest taste, with all kinds of cake and fruit, placed undesired in an apartment we were to go through, which, as the family were from home, I thought was very clever in the housekeeper, for one is so often asked by people whether one *chuses* chocolate, which forbidding word puts (as intended) a negative on the question.

1756

*

Burghley Hall, Northants: [We] proposed taking Burleigh Hall in our way to Stamford, tho' we feared obtaining a sight of it, the present Lord having not long been in possession. The whole was then repairing, and we had been told he was not fond of strangers seeing it while it bore so ruinous an appearance. However, we were more fortunate than we expected, for as we were walking in the gardens, standing still on a nearer approach to the house (which seems almost of itself a little town), Lord Exeter happened to be overlooking his workmen, and reading, as I suppose, curiosity in our countenances, politely asked if the ladies chose to see it, our reply being in the affirmative, he himself informed us where was the most easy entrance.

Mrs Lybbe Powys, *Diaries,* 1757

Knole Park, Kent: [We] had our cold loaf with us and eat it in the gateway.

Elizabeth, 1st Duchess of Northumberland,
Travel Journals, c. 1766

The vile custom of not being able to view a house, without paying for the sight, as if it was exhibited by a *show-man,* is detestable.

Arthur Young, *A Southern Tour,* 1767

A small white house, belonging to an old military comrade of mine, I could not in friendship pass by; so I rode up to the door. The captain was at home, but the servant said could not see me, being shut up; which he explain'd being still in bed: at 10 o'clock. I sent up my name, and enter'd the house, from which are delightful and extensive views, of the town and bridge of Monmouth.... The parlour was (ill) furnish'd in the modern taste, with French chairs, festoon'd curtains, and puff'd bell ropes; this and his keeping in bed informed me that the gentleman was not master of his own house; at length (in a loose bed gown) he appear'd; then never gave me an invitation to stay, or could possibly ride a mile with me, for his wife being big with child, he never stirr'd abroad. *Risum teneatis Amici!*

5th Viscount Torrington, *Diaries*, 16.6.1781

Holland House

Luton Hoo, Bedfordshire: As we entered the Park, I talked in a high style of my old friendship with Lord Mount Stuart, and said, 'I shall probably be much at this place.' The Sage, aware of human vicissitudes, gently checked me. 'Don't you be too sure of that.'

James Boswell, *The Life of Samuel Johnson*, 1781

Wroxton Abbey, Oxfordshire : When we had climb'd the hill we passed by the seat of the late Mr Child [Upton House]; and in a few miles came to Wroxton where Ld Guildford has an old seat and I prevail'd upon my party to drive down to it: when unluckily for us Ld G was just arrived from London and denied us admittance. Very rude this and unlike an old courtly lord! Let him either forbid his place entirely; open it allways; or else fix a day of admission: but, for shame, don't refuse travellers who may have come 20 miles out of their way for a sight of the place.

8.7.1785

❋

Blenheim Palace, Oxfordshire : Mr C went with me to the house, following a great crowd, which we hoped wou'd soon pass away; and in the interim, I got a sight of the China room, well fill'd I believe, and with several elegant services; after we enter'd the hall, we fell in with a corps of 30 observers – what a plague and fatigue! However we travelled through the rooms, and were shewn the great works of Rubens, which are, in my eyes, disgusting and indecent.

16.8.1787

❋

Chatsworth, Derbyshire : came to Edinsor Inn in the village of that name; there leaving our horses, and ordering dinner, we walk'd back to Chatsworth; where the porter was *so obliging* as to find the gardener, and the housekeeper for us; who are always *ready* to attend to strangers.

14.6.1789

❋

Haddon Hall, Derbyshire : now quite dismantled, and the timber fell'd. . . . The farmer who inhabits the farm near the Gate (part of the old out houses) most civilly put up my nag; and then attended me. . . .

This poor abandon'd place is totally deserted . . .
The old kitchen is woefully damp. 'Aye', said the
farmer, "twou'd kill a fly in five minutes in summer! . . .'
In a room, below, hung with tatter'd tapestry, call'd
the wardrobe, are many remains of rusty armour. 'Sr,'
quoth the farmer (my intelligent guide), 'many gentlemen will stay hours in this house, and prefer the obser-
vation here to the being in Chatsworth.' 'That's just
my case.' 'And some, Sr, will desire to take away pieces
of armour.' 'That I shou'd like to do too.' 'Why then,
Sr, as you seem fond of these things, there is a sword
hilt, with part of the blade, said to be worn by the
Vernons in the wars of France'; and so I instantly
carried him off.

15.6.1789

*

Lyme Park, Derbyshire : I stood before the house, when
my lady housekeeper came out – in civility, as I
thought, so I said, 'Is there any family here?' 'Yes, to
be sure.' 'Mr Legh's?' 'No.' 'Then I can see the
house?' 'Indeed you can't; I should have enough to do
then.' 'Pleasing business, surely for a housekeeper?'
'We never show it but to those we know.' 'Then I am
happy not to be able to see it.'

Thus we parted in mutual contempt; tho' it seems
to be so miserable a house, that she would not be over-
fatigued.

5th Viscount Torrington, *Diaries*, 26.6.1792

Piercefield House, Monmouthshire : We entered Pierce-
field Walk which winds along the top of the Cliff
having beneath the river Wye. We stopped at several
openings where there are seats. . . . Having brought
provisions with us we dined at the entrance of a sub-
terranean passage cut through the rock.

Not having knives and forks and glasses we sent to
Pierce-field House and were furnished with them.

[*Which seems an extraordinary liberty considering that the owner was unknown to them.*] . . . We walked past the House which is a specimen of very bad taste in architecture.

J. Farington, *Diary*, Vol. II, 16.9.1803

Woburn Abbey, Bedfordshire: Set off at half past seven o'clock . . . passed a handsome gateway on the right, the entrance into Woburn Park, but they would not allow us to enter that way, so we had to go two miles further by the Park Wall, till we came to the town. Drove to the George Inn, wrote to the House-keeper and got leave to see the Abbey. About ten o' clock set off for Woburn Abbey. We drove two miles through the grounds before we reached the House and then passed between two high walls. [*When they finally got inside the house they were passed through the rooms by one porter to another.*] One small room appropriated to Maps. The Duke's Librarian and Chaplain were at their studies.

Anne Rushout, unpublished diaries, 25.7.1822

Stratfield Saye, Hampshire: Those desirous of seeing the Interior of the House, are requested to ring at the door of entrance and to express their desire. It is wished that the practice of stopping on the paved walk to look in at the windows should be discontinued.

Noticeboard worded by the 1st Duke of Wellington and placed at the front door, *c.* 1825-40

Demolition

Country houses have been demolished throughout the centuries. The difference between the past ages and the present age is that those country houses pulled down in the

*former were often replaced by better ones, whereas those
pulled down in the latter are replaced only by rubble.*

My ancient manor-house, that's noted for good eating,
demolished to build up a modern kickshaw like my
Lord Courstair's seat about a mile off, with sashes,
pictures and china, but never any victuals dressed in
the house for fear the smoke of the chimney should
sully the nice furniture.

T. Baker, *Tunbridge Wells*, 1703

Foolish people, builders and workmen and some times
stewards are always for pulling down because they get
by it. And people that are young and have no experience
are often drawn into extravagant expenses to make
their house worse.

Sarah, Duchess of Marlborough to Diana,
Duchess of Bedford, 4.7.1732

Canons Park, Middlesex : Yesterday I went in greet
state in a coach and four early in the morning to visit
the Duke of Chandois's noble palece at Canons, which,
alas! is now to be sold purely to be demolished for the
sake of the beautiful materials. The edifice has already
suffered for want of its lord, & within quite upon the
decline, methinks I see vast havock among vases,
statues, some of which are already fallen to the ground,
the tearing down of the fine painted ceilings, the work
of Leguere, the noble stuckos, & gildings, which must
be all anulled into common mortar, & in a few days
fluted marble Ionic colums, bustos, pictures, & well
carved marble chimney pieces, will be all dissipated
to the 4 quarters of the island; the Chapel, I believe
will be destroyed. Alas! I lament the fate of the
glorious painted windows with sacred story richely
dighte, casting a dim religious lighte, & the well turned
again now struck dumb. . . .

Samuel Gale to William Stukeley, 16.5.1747
(*Memorials of Stukeley*, Vol. I, Surtees Society, Vol. 73, 1882)

Westhorpe Hall, Bucks: I went to see the dismal ruins of Westhorpe Hall, formerly the seat of Charles Brandon, Duke of Suffolk. The workmen are now pulling it down as fast as may be in a very careless and injudicious manner. . . . But all the time chimnies and ornaments were pulled down with ropes, and crushed to pieces in a most shameful manner. There was a monstruous figure of Hercules sitting cross-legged, with a club and lyon by him, but all shattered to pieces; and the painted glass is like to share the same fate. . . . It is a pity but some care was taken to preserve some few of our ancient fabricks, as they do at Rome, but to demolish every piece of old architecture is quite barbarous.

Horace Walpole, 1787

Here mouldering fanes and battlements arise,
    Turrets and arches nodding to their fall,
Unpeopled monast'ries delude our eyes,
    And mimic desolation covers all.

'Ah!' said the sighing peer, 'had Bute been true,
    Nor Mungo's, Rigby's, Bradshaw's friendship vain,
Far better scenes than these had blest our view,
    And realized the beauties which we feign:

Purged by the sword, and purified by fire,
    Then had we seen proud London's hated walls;
Owls would have hooted in St Peter's choir,
    And foxes stunk and litter'd in St Paul's.

Thomas Gray, 'Impromptu, suggested by a view, in 1766,
Of the Seat and Ruins of a Deceased Nobleman, at
Kingsgate, Kent'

'Unpeopled monast'ries' – It is a fact that the dissolution of the monasteries in sixteenth-century England marked the end of the Middle Ages and the exhaustion of a social system which had flourished for centuries. Tragic though the demolition of the beautiful monastic buildings was,

*in their place arose the no less beautiful country houses.
For four hundred consecutive years they survived and the
country was virtually governed by the squires in place of
the monks. Now this social system has given way to
another. We must hope that the new social system, when
stabilized, will eventually be symbolized by some new and
worthy architecture.*

*Immediately after our Civil War, when conditions were
at a very low ebb, a Leicestershire baronet was sustained
by courage, faith, and hope. He added a chapel to his
house and erected a tablet to record his motives.*

When all things sacred were throughout ye Nation
Either demolisht or profaned Sir Robert Shirley
Barronet Founded this Church whose singular praise
it is to have done ye best things in ye worst times And
hoped them in the most callamitous.

Tablet over the west door of the chapel, Staunton Harold,
Leicestershire, 1655

Acknowledgements

I am grateful to Michael Bloch, John Cornforth, John Harris Hugh Honour, and John Kenworthy-Browne for some suggestions for this anthology.

The editor and publishers gratefully acknowledge permission to use copyright material in this book:

Elizabeth Bowen: From *Bowen's Court*. By permission of Alfred A. Knopf, Inc., and Virago Press, Ely House, Dover St., London.

Lady Diana Cooper: From *The Rainbow Comes and Goes* (1958). By permission of the author.

Alice Fairfax-Lucy: From *Charlecote and the Lucys*, © Oxford University Press, 1958. By permission of Oxford University Press.

Robin Fedden: From *The Continuing Purpose* (Longman, 1968). By permission of Mrs Renée Fedden.

Mark Girouard: From *Life in the English Country House* (Yale University Press, 1978). By permission of the publisher (London).

Joyce Godber: From *The Marchioness Grey of Wrest Park* (1968). By permission of the Bedfordshire Historical Record Society.

Earl of Ilchester: Extracts from *Elizabeth Lady Holland to her Son 1821–46* (John Murray, 1945) and from *Lord Hervey and his Friends 1726–38* (John Murray, 1950) both edited by the Earl of Ilchester. By permission of the publisher.

James Lees-Milne: Extract from *Prophesying Peace*. Copyright © 1977 by James Lees-Milne (London: Chatto and Windus, 1977; New York: Charles Scribner's Sons, 1977). Extract from *Ancestral Voices*. Copyright © 1975 by James Lees-Milne (London: Chatto and Windus, 1975; New York: Charles Scribner's Sons, 1975). By permission of the publishers. Extract from *Earls of Creation* (Hamish Hamilton, 1962). By permission of the publisher. Extract from *English Country Houses, Baroque* (Hamlyn, 1970). By permission of the publisher.

Lady Emily Lutyens: From *A Blessed Girl* (Hart-Davis, 1953). By permission of Granada Publishing Ltd.

The National Trust for Places of Historic Interest or Natural Beauty for permission to reprint an extract from the guidebook to *Claydon House, 1974*.

ACKNOWLEDGEMENTS

Sylas Neville: From *The Diary of Sylas Neville, 1767–1788*, edited by Bazil Cozens-Hardy (1950). By permission of Oxford University Press.

Harold Nicolson: Extracts from *Helen's Tower* (1937), *Diary*, and from 'The Edwardian Weekend' in *Small Talk* (1937). By permission of Nigel Nicolson, Literary Executor to Sir Harold Nicolson.

V. Sackville-West: From *The Edwardians* (Hogarth Press, 1930). Reprinted by permission of Curtis Brown Ltd., London, on behalf of the Estate of Victoria Sackville-West and of Avon Books.

Georgiana Caroline Sitwell: From 'The Dew it lies on the Wood' in *Two Generations* by Osbert Sitwell (Macmillan, 1940).

Osbert Sitwell: From *The Scarlet Tree* (Macmillan, 1946). By permission of David Higham Associates Ltd.

Francis Thompson: From *Chatsworth: A Short History* (Country Life, 1951).

Evelyn Waugh: Extracts from *Brideshead Revisited* (Chapman & Hall, 1945) and from *A Handful of Dust* (Chapman & Hall, 1934). By permission of A. D. Peters & Co., Ltd.

Denton Welch: From *Journals* (Hamish Hamilton, 1946). By permission of David Higham Associates Ltd.

Duchess of Windsor: From *The Heart has its Reasons* (Michae Joseph, 1956).

While every effort has been made to secure permission we may have failed in a few cases to trace the copyright holder. We apologize for any apparent negligence.

The illustrations in this book were taken from the following sources: Jane Austen, *Mansfield Park* (London, 1902); Harry Carter, *Orlando Jewitt* (London, 1962); Robert W. Edis, *Decoration & Furniture of Town Houses* (London, 1881); Herbert A. Evans, *Highways and Byways in Oxford and the Cotswolds* (London, 1924); Charles G. Harper, *Cycle Rides Round London* (London, 1902); William Howitt, *Homes and Haunts of the Most Eminent British Poets* Volume I (London, 1847); Frederick Litchfield, *Illustrated History of Furniture* (London, 1892); Mrs Orrinsmith, *The Drawing-Room* (London, 1878); A. J. Quiller-Couch, *The Warwickshire Avon* (London, 1892); M. H. Spielmann and Walter Jerrold, *Hugh Thomson* (London, 1931); Irving Zucker, *A Source Book of French Advertising Art* (London, 1970).

Index